A BEACON FOR THE BLIND

LECTOR HOUSE PUBLIC DOMAIN WORKS

A BEACON FOR THE BLIND

WINIFRED HOLT,
JAMES BRYCE

ISBN: 978-93-90294-08-4

Published: 1914

LECTOR HOUSE LLP
E-MAIL: lectorpublishing@gmail.com

PROFESSOR AND MRS. FAWCETT

From the painting by Ford Madox Brown, now in the National Portrait Gallery

A BEACON FOR THE BLIND

BEING A LIFE OF HENRY FAWCETT THE BLIND POSTMASTER-GENERAL

BY

WINIFRED HOLT

WITH A FOREWORD BY HON. VISCOUNT BRYCE

'He that is greatest among you
let him be servant of all.'

1914

THIS BOOK IS DEDICATED
TO THE FIVE ON TWO CONTINENTS
WHO MADE ITS WRITING POSSIBLE——
IN ENGLAND, B. T. AND F. DE G. E.
IN AMERICA, E. H. B., H. H.
AND R. H.

FOREWORD BY THE
RIGHT HON. VISCOUNT BRYCE
LATE BRITISH AMBASSADOR TO AMERICA

There has been no more striking example in our time of how self-reliance and strength of purpose can triumph over adverse fortune than that presented by the career of Henry Fawcett. The story of his life as it is to be told in this book will give ample illustrations of his fortitude and his perseverance. All that I, an old friend of his, need speak of is a quality hardly less remarkable than was his energy. I mean his cheerfulness. It was specially wonderful and admirable in one afflicted as he was. Nothing would seem so to cut a man off from his fellows as the loss of sight, nor would it appear possible to enjoy the charms of external nature without seeing them. Fawcett, however, delighted in society. He never moped. He loved to be among his friends, and found an inexhaustible pleasure in talk wherever he was, in his College (Trinity Hall, Cambridge), at London dinner-parties, in the lobbies or smoking-room of the House of Commons. If he had moments of sadness in solitude we knew nothing of them, for in company he was always bright. His greetings were joyous; his good spirits proverbial at Cambridge, and indeed in all the circles that knew him, making his friends feel, in any moments of depression that might come upon them, half ashamed to be less cheery than one with whom fate had dealt so hardly. Without this natural buoyancy of temper, even such a resolute will as his might have failed to achieve so much as he achieved. He seemed determined to hold on to every possible source of enjoyment he had ever known before sight was lost. That determination used to strike me most in his fondness for open-air nature and physical exercise. He loved not only walking but riding. I remember how once when I was staying with him in the same country house in Surrey, our host arranged a long excursion on horseback through the lanes and woods of the pretty country that lies on both sides of the North Downs, to the south-west of London. Fawcett insisted on being one of the party, and when he approached a place where the bridle-path ran through a wood of beeches, whose spreading boughs came down almost to the height of the horses' heads, he said to me, 'Tell me to duck my head whenever we come to a spot where the branches are low.' I felt uneasy, for if he had struck against one of the thick boughs, he might have been unhorsed and would certainly have been hurt. However, I went in front and warned him as he had desired. He rode on fearlessly, stooping low over the horse's neck whenever I called out to him to do so, and he evidently enjoyed the fresh scent of the woods and the rustling of the leaves just as much as did all the rest of us.

His love of nature, joined to his sympathy with the masses of the people, made him eager to secure the preservation of public rights in commons and village greens and footpaths. He was one of the founders of that Commons Preservation Society which has done so much to save open spaces in England from the grasp of the spoiler; frequently attended its meetings, and was always ready to vote and speak in the House of Commons when any question involving popular rights in the land arose there.

At a time when extremely few non-official persons in Parliament interested themselves in the government and administration of India, Fawcett, though he had never visited the East, and had no family connection with it, felt, and set himself to impress upon others, the grave responsibility of Britain for the welfare of the peoples of India. He studied with characteristic thoroughness and assiduity the facts and conditions of Indian life, the financial problems those conditions involve, the needs and feelings of the subject population. His speeches were of the greatest value in calling public attention to these subjects, and his name is gratefully remembered in India.

His mental powers were remarkable rather for strength than for subtlety. It was an eminently English intellect, forcible in its broad commonsense way of looking at things, and in its disposition to pass by side issues and refinements in order to go straight to the main conclusions he desired to enforce. This was what chiefly gave weight to his speeches in Parliament and on the platform. Debarred as he was from the use of writing, he formed the habit of thinking out fully beforehand both what he meant to say and the words in which he meant to say it, and thus he became a master of lucid statement and cogent argument, making each of his points sharp and clear, and driving them home in a way which every listener could comprehend. The same merits of directness and coherency are conspicuous in his writings on political economy, his favourite study. There were no dark corners in his mind any more than in his political creed, or indeed in his course of action as a statesman. In practical politics, it was said of him, to use a familiar phrase, that you always knew where to find him. That was one of the qualities which secured for him not only the confidence of his political friends but the respect of his political opponents. When he died prematurely he had reached a position in the House of Commons which would have secured his early admission to the Cabinet, and the only doubt I ever heard raised was whether his blindness, which would have made it necessary that documents, however confidential, should be read aloud to him, would have constituted a fatal obstacle.

The force of his character and the vigour of his intellect must have ensured him a distinguished career even had he been stricken by no calamity. That he should have been stricken by one which would have overwhelmed almost any other man, and should have triumphed over it by his cheerful and persistent courage, marks him out as an extraordinary man, worthy to be long remembered.

BRYCE.

CONTENTS

YOUTH

CHAPTER I

WATERLOO, THE MAYOR, AND THE BABY

CHAPTER II

THE BOY LECTURER

CAMBRIDGE

CHAPTER III

THE TALL STUDENT

CHAPTER IV

A SET BACK

WINNING BACK

CHAPTER V

DARKNESS

CHAPTER VI

HAPPINESS

CHAPTER VII

DISTRACTION

CAMBRIDGE AGAIN

CHAPTER VIII

THE PROBLEM OF THE POOR

CHAPTER IX

THE GOOD SAMARITAN

CHAPTER X

THE YOUNG ECONOMIST

THE PROFESSOR OF POLITICAL ECONOMY

THE NEW M.P.

CHAPTER XVIII

GLADSTONE PRIME MINISTER

SAVING THE PEOPLE'S PLAYGROUNDS

CHAPTER XIX

THE STOLEN COMMONS

CHAPTER XX

THE FIGHT FOR THE FOREST

CHAPTER XXI

FOR THE PEOPLE'S WOODS AND STREAMS

THE MEMBER FOR INDIA

CHAPTER XXII

WHAT INDIA PAID

CHAPTER XXIII

THE 'ONE MAN WHO CARED FOR INDIA'

CHAPTER XXIV

FAMINE, TURKS AND INDIANS

A NEW KIND OF POSTMASTER-GENERAL

CHAPTER XXV

LIBERALS IN POWER

CHAPTER XXVI

FRESH AIR, BLUE RIBBONS, AND POSTMEN

CHAPTER XXVII

THE PENNIES OF THE POOR

A TRIUMPHANT END

CHAPTER XXVIII

AT HOME AND AT COURT

CHAPTER XXIX

A GRAVE ILLNESS

CHAPTER XXX

AMONG THE BLIND

CHAPTER XXXI

LIGHT

LIST OF ILLUSTRATIONS

INTRODUCTION

'I wish we had Fawcett here to-day. At this crisis England needs him sorely.' These words, said with much feeling by the late Lord Avebury, were spoken to the writer of this book only two years ago.

Fawcett is not needed only in England. His is the type of man needed sorely to-day and every day in every empire and democracy under the sun. His example of valour against odds is just as necessary for America as for the Mother Country, for the men who are now doing the world's work as for the lads who will be at work to-morrow.

Sir Leslie Stephen said that while writing the biography of Fawcett, there was not a single fact which he had to conceal, nothing to explain away, nothing to apologise for, and he judged the best way to do his subject honour was to tell the plain story as fully and as frankly as he could.

Sir Leslie wrote with the reticent dignity of one recently grieving for the loss of his friend; the present writer will have executed her task if she has succeeded in throwing a more personal light on the heroic figure of Fawcett.

This little book has no pretensions. It endeavours merely to preserve carefully and reverently glimpses and flashes—which might have otherwise been lost—of a great life, a life of deep significance not only to those who see, but especially to those who, like Fawcett, must depend for their vision on that inner eye which no calamity can darken.

When he lost his sight, Fawcett had his fixed manner of life, his tastes and ambitions, and he was painfully forced to readjust himself to altered aspects. The tracing of the beneficent effect of this necessity on a man of his strong mind, body and will, is a psychological study of deep interest.

His attitude towards questions that are still vital, such as the treatment of dependent peoples, the widening of the suffrage and the perfecting of its machinery, make his personality still unique, modern and absorbing.

A nearer view of the man, seen through the recollections and anecdotes of his friends, shows his intense love of fun, his high ideals and bravery, his tremendous industry and accomplishment.

The author is grateful for permission to use the facsimiles of the letters of Queen Victoria and the Prince of Wales (King Edward).

She is also deeply obliged for the help given by reminiscences and anecdotes from the Right Honourable the late Lord Avebury; Dr. Beck, Master of Trinity

Hall, Cambridge; Dr. Henry Bond; the Right Honourable Viscount Bryce, late British Ambassador to America; Sir Francis Campbell; the late Robert Campbell, Esq.; the Honourable Joseph H. Choate, late American Ambassador to Great Britain; Lord and Lady Courtney; Sir Alfred Dale; the late Sir Robert Hunter; the late Sir William Lee-Warner, G.C.S.I.; the Right Honourable Viscount Morley; Lady Ritchie, Miss McCleod Smith; the Right Honourable the late James Stuart, Esq., and Mr. Sedley Taylor.

She is particularly indebted to Miss Fawcett, the sister of Mr. Fawcett, and to Mrs. Fawcett, his widow, for their assistance. Their interest in the book was a great stimulus towards its writing. Mr. F. J. Dryhurst, C.B., who from 1871 to 1884 was secretary to Mr. Fawcett, has been a great aid in preparing the book. The greatest assistance has been given by Miss de Grasse Evans and Miss Beatrice Taylor, without whose sympathy and help in various stages of the work its completion might have been impossible.

It has been inevitable that Sir Leslie's biography should be largely quarried. His arrangement of facts has been followed as the simplest and most logical framework for the story, and descriptions of scenes which he and his friends witnessed, and stories of Fawcett not elsewhere given, have been used. The admiration and gratitude of the novice for help from the master biographer is here humbly recorded.

This book should enhance the interest of the older biography, which perhaps may be reintroduced after many years oblivion—as it has been out of print—by its younger and less formal companion.

The material to be had has been used and adapted as it might best serve, and the narrative has not been interrupted to give its source; it is believed that this policy will be in accordance with the wishes of those of Mr. Fawcett's appreciators who have so generously helped.

The more we know about this brave, patient and humorous man, the more inspiration we get; and to help us to achieve and to rejoice—never was inspiration more sorely needed than to-day! It is in the hope of supplying a little of this great need that this brief story of a steadfast life is written.

WINIFRED HOLT.

YOUTH

'Where the pools are bright and deep,
Where the gray trout lies asleep,
Up the river and over the lea,
That's the way for Billy and me.'

James Hogg.

CHAPTER I

WATERLOO, THE MAYOR, AND THE BABY

The Fisherman—The Battle of Waterloo—The Mayor of Salisbury—
The Mayor's Son—The Market-place—The Circus—Boarding-School and Fun—A Diary.

One midsummer day in 1815 a young draper's assistant was gently fishing in
the Salisbury Avon. William Fawcett was but lately come to Salisbury, yet he already knew his river. While trying a deep pool in the shadow of a bridge near the
town he was startled by shouts from the roadway above. 'News from the army! A
great victory! Boney in flight!'

The fisherman forgot his fish, and hurried away to join the rejoicing crowd
gathering in the market-place. There having been bustled to the roof of a stage-
coach, and had the gazette containing the news thrust into his hands, he read out
in his remarkably clear and resonant voice the account of the great battle of Waterloo.

Rejoicings.

Seventeen years later, when the shopkeeper had become the Mayor of Salisbury, he again led the town in rejoicings. The great Reform Bill had become law.
Salisbury townsfolk were henceforth to have a voice in the councils of the nation,
and the barren hill on which stood the pocket borough of old Sarum was no longer
to mock them with its political power.

The town joyously prepared to celebrate the event. The houses were decorated. Elaborate illuminations were set up. Victory, assisted by Greek gods and
goddesses, presided over a transparency in which Britannia throttled the hydra of
corruption, while Wellington and Peel scowled in the background. Meat and beer
were given to the poor; in the market-place, at great fires lighted in the open air,
whole sheep were roasted. The smoke swirled blindly about the bustling crowd,
and then surged up past the latticed windows of the Mayor's house, to seek in ever
thinning rifts the spire of the wonderful cathedral that for centuries has watched
over the destinies of the town. The next day was held in the market-place a great
banquet, at which the Mayor presided; and after dinner all adjourned to the Green
Croft Cricket Ground, where his Worship led off the dance with a prominent and
elderly lady of the town—the Mayor resplendent in plaited shirt frill and high
stock, the buckles on his shoes twinkling as he cut 'pigeon wings,' the lady sedate
in her wide brocade gown, her poke bonnet, and lace veil.

Fawcett's heart was as light as his heels on that occasion. All his life he had been a reformer, a staunch Liberal, ardent for the extension of the franchise. It says much for his personal charm and worth that, in a close Tory borough such as Salisbury then was, he should have been chosen Mayor by his political opponents.

The Mayor and his Wife.

So dear to his heart was the spirit of freedom that the Mayor had forsooth to fall in love with the daughter of the solicitor who acted as agent for the Liberal party. Miss Mary Cooper was a good and clever woman, deeply interested in politics, and as ardent a reformer as the man she married.

The couple were sociable and humorous. They kept a good table, laid in an excellent stock of wine, and diffused such a pleasant atmosphere of hospitality that they became immensely popular, and many distinguished people sought their company. But William Fawcett was not only a good townsman, he was a good countryman as well, a great jumper, a keen sportsman, a good shot, and a renowned fisherman.

The Brick-house Baby.

In 1833, when the Princess Victoria was fourteen years old, when the negro slaves were being freed throughout the British Colonies, when Stephenson had completed his locomotive and the first railroads had been started, when all things seemed to be pushing and striving for independence and progress, in the Mayor's old low red-brick house overlooking the market-place, in a wonderful Elizabethan room, on 26th August, Henry Fawcett was born.

The baby seems to have been singularly like most other babies. He shared the uneventful placidity of his nursery with an older brother, William, and a sister, Sarah Maria. Six years later there came another brother, Thomas Cooper.

The Market.

When Harry was four years old Queen Victoria, whom he was to serve in so distinguished a capacity, came to the throne. But it was still too early to find in Harry indications of the future statesman. He was delicate, and much spoiled at home, had a strong will of his own, and was on the whole rather selfish. He was not an imaginative child, though he loved at times, holding his sister Maria tightly by the hand, to venture into the great cathedral and see the coloured light as it filtered through the high windows, or to thrill in response to the thundering of the great organ. But more often we find him, still very tiny, standing squarely on his feet, inquiring with real interest the price of bacon, how much sheep and wool brought; or walking with his father and wearying him with ceaseless economic questions as to 'Why are things cheaper to-day than last month?' 'Why does butter cost more than milk?' until that patient man was heard to exclaim not too patiently, 'Harry asks me so many questions that he quite worries me.'

HENRY FAWCETT'S MOTHER

He went to a Dame's school, where his first teacher said that she had never had so troublesome a pupil, that his head was like a colander; but Harry puts the case more pathetically when he tells his mother that 'Mrs. Harris says if we go on, we shall kill her, and we do go on,' regretfully adding, 'and yet she does not die.' A schoolmate of these days says that Harry lisped very much, and that the boys used to tease him about it. He was also so slow about his lessons that they called him thickhead. But when school was out Harry entered the realms he loved. From his home on the market-place he had only to go outside the door to be at once in touch with the active world whose economic problems appealed to him so keenly. He made friends among the country folk, and talked of their crops and the money they would bring, and noted in his childish mind the rise and fall in the price of wheat.

The Circus.

Then to the same open space came all sorts of travelling shows. Sometimes the circus spread its mysterious tents, and when the children were dragged away from the wild beasts and the seductive freaks and put to bed, the little Fawcetts would stealthily creep to the bedroom window overlooking the market and see the lights shining on all the wonderful but forbidden marvels, and hear the hurdy-gurdy and the band mix their triumphal blare with the solemn striking of the clock in the near-by cathedral.

Boarding-School.

In 1841 Harry's father took a delightful farmhouse at Longford, about three miles south of Salisbury, with delectable streams full of fish. Harry loved to fish every day, and hated lessons, but, alas! grim fate backed the lessons, and sent him ruthlessly to school. He went as a boarder to Mr. Sopp at Alderbury, a few miles away.

There are many tales showing that Harry loved the fleshpots and that he had been much indulged at home. He writes, 'I have begun Ovid—I hate it.' 'This is a beastly school—milk and water, no milk—bread and butter, no butter. Please give a quarter's notice.'

And still more heartrending was the prayer to his mother, 'Please when the family has quite finished with the ham bone, send it to me.' Imagination can supply the effect of this on the family circle, and guess what a well-covered ham bone was shipped to the starving Harry. Starving or no, he grew immensely stronger and larger, and though he never admitted that he got enough to eat at any school, he became ultimately reconciled to his exile.

He used to come home often for half-holidays, and to go to Longford and revel in all country delights. Then began the close friendships with the cottagers about him which meant so much to him and influenced all his life.

In the summer that completed his tenth year there came to Salisbury two men who also loved the common people and sought to make their lives easier. It was the year of the great Free Trade campaign in the agricultural districts, and the men were Cobden and Bright. They visited Harry's father, and perhaps Harry himself met them then for the first time. Lord Morley has said in his life of Cobden that 'the picture of these two men, leaving their homes and their business, and going over the length and breadth of the land to convert the nation, had about it something apostolic.' In a home where they and their teachings were so reverenced, to even hear of their journeyings would make a strong impression on a boy of Harry's interests, and perhaps helped to give a definite aim to his ambitions.

At Mr. Sopp's school he began a diary, of which the penmanship is admirable. On some days the only record is the startling fact, 'It was a very fine day.' June 21st, 1847, however, is a very eventful day, for he lists the capture of the first fish that he took with a fly, which weighed 'about three-quarters of a pound.'

Hedgehogs and Cake.

Again, he is transported with joy by the gift of a hedgehog and four young ones, and he has a glorious time in going on board H.M.S. *Howe*, of one hundred and twenty guns. On one occasion he goes to the theatre, on another he is in court hearing a trial. He begins Greek, and this anguish is modified by the arrival of a cake for one of his schoolfellows, which Harry doubtless shares.

A change of scene is recorded in the diary when on 3rd August Henry becomes the first pupil at Queenwood College. In its previous career this temple of learning had been Harmony Hall, built by Robert Owen for his last socialist experiment. In 1817 it was opened as a school by Mr. Edmonson, a Quaker. Special emphasis was given to scientific training and English literature. The school seems to have been very congenial to Harry, and his intellect now began to develop rapidly.

The Editor.

To continue from the diary, we learn that 'we elected the various school officers. J. Mansergh and I were elected without opposition editors of the *Queenwood Chronicle.*' He had been at Queenwood but a fortnight, and was fourteen years old when this great honour came to him. Mr. Fawcett was delighted at this good news, and offered because of it and because Harry had been 'studying most determinedly' to take the boy to Stonehenge. His aversion to books had distressed his family, and this new interest in his studies gave his father great pleasure. On reading a composition which Harry had sent home, Mr. Fawcett exclaimed to his wife, 'I really think, mother, after all that there is something in that boy!' His literary performances at this time indicate an increasing imagination, but in the main he never deviated from the practical paths of thought shown when as a tiny child he studiously investigated the Salisbury market. His schoolmates report him as 'tall for his age, loose-limbed, and rather ungainly.' He had become much of a bookworm, and though later good at games, at this time he preferred to wander off by himself and read. He was strongest in mathematics; languages did not much appeal to him; but he liked to learn long passages of poetry by heart. There was a disused chalk-pit near Queenwood where he would take refuge and declaim his lines. The extravagance of his gesticulations might well cause unexpecting passers-by to consider him the village loony.

CHAPTER II

THE BOY LECTURER

A Lecture on the uses of Steam—Parliamentary Ambitions—King's
College—Politics in the Fifties—Cribbage and Cricket.

Fawcett was interested in the scientific lectures, and he had a very good time. Professor Tyndall took them out surveying. Harry comments on a lecture at which he heard that there 'is fire in everything, even ice'; he also records some chemical experiments in the laboratory.

In September the diary states, 'I began writing my lecture on phonography, on the uses of steam without copying any of it.'

There is an error here, as these were two lectures, not one. That on steam, in a blue marbled-covered copy-book, lies before the writer. The title, inscribed in tall, shaded handwriting, contained within scrupulously ruled lines, is:

=====================================

A Lecture delivered by H. Fawcett
On Uses of Steam
At Queenwood College
September 27, 1847.

=====================================

The ink, which was black sixty-six years ago, is now much faded; but the essay of the fourteen-year-old schoolboy is still fresh and interesting, and so prophetic of the man that it is like a simple map indicating the chief features of the country we are about to see.

Henry writes in his careful penmanship, for which he must have been marked at least 9+ in a scale of 10, 'Things which appear simple to an unobserving Person are to an observing Person the most complicated and beautifully formed ... such a simple Thing as a blade of Grass, has ever any Man been yet so wise as to tell what it is?'

The Essayist.

Here is another curious sentence written by the bright-eyed youngster with the monumental dignity of the lecturer:

'What can be so beautifully contrived and framed as the human Body, where there are innumerable Parts, acting all in Unity?... if one of the Parts go wrong, the whole Body is put out of Tune ... is there any one Part of our Body which we could dispense with?... I think the Answer "No" must be evident to every one.'

It is curious that Fawcett should have been called upon later by the loss of his eyesight to contradict this childish statement, and to prove not only that we can get along without some of our most precious faculties, but that the law of compensation so works that we may be able to accomplish more by reason of the loss.

The essay proceeds to deal with railways, and contains all kinds of figures relating to tonnage, trains, traffics, the cost of railroad construction, etc., all with careful, correct figures; a complicated study for a railroad expert. This schoolboy is already coping with the figures and statistics of which he had later such a marvellous control. He dwells on the importance of the railroad to the Wiltshire farmer, who can sell his cheese at sevenpence a pound in London, when it is only worth sixpence where it is made. In this and similar statements we find the political economist foreshadowed: he speaks of the nobility who selfishly object to having railways, which he feels are the greatest help to the common people; and he adds, 'A Man should sacrifice a little of his own Pleasure when he knows that by sacrificing that Pleasure he will benefit the People at large.' We must note that pleasure is always spelt with a beautiful and exceptionally large P.

Later there are some intelligent remarks on the power of a railway to create traffic, so that 'some Railways have been made between two Places where there was not sufficient Traffic for a Coach, and yet when they are made, a Trade springs up, and they pay very well indeed.'

Transporta-tion — Rich and Poor.

He further approves of the railway as a means of cheap transportation, and remarks, 'Many a Person can avail himself of a Day's Pleasure ...' or, 'Enjoy the beautiful Air of some Country Village.' Here we have not only the keystone of Henry Fawcett's character, but indications of the political activities in which he was to be so pre-eminent. His public career was one long, unbroken effort to do away with the monopolies and prerogatives of any class, and so to increase the independence and rights of the poor.

The essay continues by quoting from an article in the *Quarterly Review* written in 1825, which considers it impossible that an engine could travel eighteen miles an hour. With evident joy he quotes, 'The gross Exaggerations of the Powers of the Locomotive Steam Engine, or to speak English, the Steam Carriage, may delude for a time, but must end in Mortification to those concerned. We should as soon expect the People of Woolwich to suffer themselves to be fired off in Congreve's Ricochet Rockets, as to trust themselves to the Mercies of such a Machine going at such a rate.' Harry himself then tells of the M.P. who insisted that the best possible locomotive could not compete with a canal boat. The scribe seems fully to appreciate the humour of this, and so foreshadows the love of fun and the vibrant laugh of the man to be.

Steam-engines lead to steamships. Our author now invites us to cross 'the wide heaving Ocean,' saying, 'When you are on a Voyage in a Steam Vessel you feel none of that Inconvenience of having to remain at Anchor for two or three Weeks waiting for a favourable Wind ... you can proceed, for you are quite independent of the Winds, and the Speed of a Steam Vessel is very considerably greater than that of any other Vessel.' A steam vessel went from Liverpool to Boston in eleven days and nine hours, and yet when steam navigation was struggling into existence 'it struck the minds of our brave Captains as a poor mean mechanical Thing unworthy of the least Consideration.'... 'I think you may almost remark' (note the conservative discretion) 'that the greatest and most useful inventions when they are struggling into Existence receive the greatest Opposition, because they make great changes, and most people, especially the ignorant, are generally very adverse to any changes.'

Patriotism — Bonaparte and Babylon.

Now he boasts magnificently about the British navy and merchant marine, approves of Bonaparte's wisdom in coveting the British sailors, and yet prudently warns all against pride, citing the lamentable consequence of lack of humility to Babylon and Nineveh. We are asked to consider the relative values of coal, diamonds, gold, and silver, and are informed that 'every Difficulty can be overcome by steady Perseverance — some Persons will never scarcely be overcome by Difficulties — they say they will do it, and they will never rest till they have performed what they want to, and it is to Men like these that we are indebted.... No Improvements or Inventions will run into a Person's Mind like Water will run into a Bottle, but they come from Years of Study and Perseverance.'

We are asked, 'Do you suppose that Sir Isaac Newton established the Laws of Gravitation without some trouble, do you suppose that such a Piece of Poetry as Milton's "Paradise Lost" was written without a Moment's Thought — or do you suppose that Watt improved the Steam Engine without some hard Labour?' Our scribe then finishes his masterpiece with a stupendous finale, by the help of a bit of poetry culled from an American newspaper and entitled the 'song of Steam,' a verse of which will be sufficient:

> 'I've no Muscle to weary, no Breast to decay,
> No Bones to be laid on the "Shelf,"
> And soon I intend you may go and play,
> While I manage the World by myself.'

This *magnum opus*, being now successfully brought to completion, is signed in full, no longer, as on the title-page, with only the initial of his first name, but by Henry Fawcett, writ exceedingly large and clear, Queenwood College, October 12th, 1847. Every page in the marbled copy-book has been filled with various spellings, and only a very few erasures, between 27th September and 12th October.

We have quoted this delicious essay as fully as space would allow, not only on account of its unique charm, but because every page is coloured by a preoccupation with those subjects and a love for those traits of human nature which were later so characteristic of Henry Fawcett, the teacher and statesman. In fact, we may accept this essay on steam as his official debut. The lecture had an encore at

Salisbury in the family circle, when, as Harry writes, all were 'much pleased with it, and Papa promised to give me a sovereign for it.'

Phonography and simplified Spelling.

His lecture on phonography is much in the spirit of to-day, when simplified spelling is causing such ardent controversies. Harry comments that 'out of fifty thousand Words in the language, only fifty are written as they are pronounced.' We must note that in these writings his own inventions in spelling tend to change these statistics.

The range of his composition at this period is great. An article on 'Angling and Sir Isaac Walton' is in happy contrast to the account of a first visit to London. Another fragment contains the acute observation that 'statesmen depend upon their brains.' In another essay called 'Reflection' an imaginary trip is taken past Spain, during which the author ponders on people who are 'made poor by gold.' Progressing to Egypt, we are told that Mahomet was 'in many respects a worthy man.' Arriving in India, our guide tells us of a company of men who, 'occupying a house of no very considerable size in London, have entirely from their enterprise and powers of mind, got possession of many thousand acres of land.' Does this refer to the East India Company, and had Harry seen the stately East India House in Leadenhall Street on that first visit to London?

The breathless exuberant feat of imagination and philosophy closes with quotations from Portia's lines to Mercy and Cicero's oration on Verres, both of which, the author truthfully says, 'show powers of reflection.'

Harry was writing and studying with a definite end in view. Already the youth had determined on a political career, and when the schoolboys discussed their plans for the future he invariably declared that he meant to be a Member of Parliament. The statement was received with roars of laughter, but Harry remained imperturbably sure.

Still at the foot of the Class.

He was at Queenwood for a year and a half, and then went to London, where he first attended King's College School, and then King's College. A schoolmate described him as 'a very tall boy with pale whitey brown hair, who always stood at the bottom of the lower sixth class.'

He attended the school in his fifteenth and sixteenth years, and then went to lectures in the college until the summer of 1852, when he was nineteen years old.

Standing in the school was, in those days, entirely determined by knowledge of the classics, for which Fawcett showed a grand indifference; but he gained the arithmetic prize in 1849, also the class-work prize, the first prize in German, and the second in French in the same term. His knowledge of these languages was always so vague that we fear his teacher was over-partial in the award, or that the other boys were strangely deficient. In 1850 he carried off another honour for mathematics, and a first prize after that in the Michaelmas term. The masters noted Fawcett's unusual mathematical power, and were also impressed by his ability to write English prose.

King's College and Cricket.

At Easter in 1851 he left school and worked only at the college for mathematics and classics. We hear that he made no particular mark; but he occasionally played billiards and cricket, and he was already an interested spectator in the gallery of the House of Commons.

During his stay in London he lived with some family connections, a Mr. and Mrs. Fearon. Mr. Fearon was a Chief Office Keeper at Somerset House, and lived there. Somerset House adjoins King's College, and this was fortunate for Harry, who, when he first went to London, had much outgrown his strength. The hours spent in the little parlour tucked away in the vast building were not without charm for the home-loving boy. Sitting on the corner of the horse-hair sofa, with its relentless early Victorian back and its unyielding springs, trying, mostly in vain, not to disturb Mrs. Fearon's best antimacassar, he would cheerfully play cribbage by the hour with his hostess, while his host expounded pungently on the questions of the day. Harry had passed from the Liberalism of the country home to the Liberalism of the metropolis. For both, Bright and Cobden were now leaders and standard-bearers, though Lord Palmerston was the Party Chief. Free Trade had been won, but neither Parliament nor country had settled down to it as a policy, and the need of another and more democratic Reform Bill was looming up on the political horizon.

These were the days that followed the abortive revolutions of '48. The battle for political independence was raging everywhere, but both leaders and rank and file were learning with bitterness to make haste slowly. None the less, hearts were glowing hotly for Freedom, and while Fawcett was in London, Kossuth, the Hungarian, was welcomed with enthusiasm. He followed Carl Schurz, that valiant apostle of Liberty, to America, where Garibaldi was already working at his soap factory on Staten Island. There was no doubt as to the heartiness of Kossuth's reception across the Atlantic. The fire of Freedom burnt to high heaven there: was it not sufficient proof of this that the dandies of that land reverently encased their mighty brains in the Kossuth hat? Talk of these great men, of their vain endeavours, of the persecution of the poor, of the need of opening cages and letting in the light of Freedom, made its mark on Harry, and he often spoke afterwards of Fearon's 'quaint and forcible' phrases.

In 1851 was the great Exhibition in Hyde Park. Did Harry's tall head peer above the crowd that lined the streets as Queen Victoria drove in state to the opening of that proud achievement? One would like to think that once with seeing eyes Fawcett beheld the little lady who presided over England's destinies throughout his working life.

And now Mr. Fawcett, senior, conscientiously counting his pennies, and the ability which his son had already shown as a student, went to his neighbour, the Dean of Salisbury. He showed the Dean Harry's mathematical papers, and asked for advice about the next step. It was not customary for one of Harry's social standing to go to a university, and the strain on the paternal purse to send him there would be considerable, but the Dean had no doubt that Cambridge offered the proper opening. The sacrifice was cheerfully made.

CAMBRIDGE

'I count life just a stuff to try the soul's strength on—educe the man.'

—Browning.

CHAPTER III

THE TALL STUDENT

Peterhouse—Quoits and Billiards—Trinity Hall—A Fellowship—Lincoln's Inn.

The new Under-graduate.

Harry knew that for his father's sake it was necessary for him to be self-supporting as soon as possible, and therefore chose his college on purely financial grounds. He went to Peterhouse, where the fellowships could be held by laymen, and were reported to be of unusual value.

His great friend, Sir Leslie Stephen, saw him there for the first time. We cannot do better than quote from Sir Leslie's biography of Fawcett the impression his subject then made upon him:

'I saw Fawcett for the first time a few months after his entrance (in October 1852).... I could point to the precise spot on the bank of the Cam where I noticed a very tall, gaunt figure swinging along with huge strides upon the towing path. He was over 6 feet 3 inches in height. His chest, I should say, was not very broad in proportion to his height, but he was remarkably large of bone and massive of limb.

'The face was impressive, though not handsome. The skull was very large; my own head vanished as into a cavern if I accidentally put on his hat. The forehead was lofty, though rather retreating, and the brow finely arched.

'The complexion was rather dull, but more than one of his early acquaintance speaks of the brightness of his eye and the keenness of his glance. The eyes were full and capable of vivid expression, though not, I think, brilliant in colour. The features were strong, and, though not delicately carved, were far from heavy, and gave a general impression of remarkable energy. The mouth long, thin-lipped, and very flexible, had a characteristic nervous tremor as of one eager to speak and voluble of discourse....

'A certain wistfulness was a frequent shade of expression. But a singularly hearty and cordial laugh constantly lighted up the whole face with an expression of most genial and infectious good-humour.[1]

'On my first glimpse of Fawcett, however, I was troubled by a question of

[1] Sir Leslie Stephen, speaking of the photograph reproduced to face p. 14, says, 'The rather peculiar expression of the eyes results from the weakness of sight presently to be noticed which made him shrink from any strong light.'

classification. I vaguely speculated as to whether he was an undergraduate, or a young farmer, or possibly somebody connected with horses at Newmarket, come over to see the sights. He had a certain rustic air, in strong contrast to that of the young Pendennises who might stroll along the bank to make a book upon the next boat race.

HENRY FAWCETT BEFORE HE WAS BLIND

'He rather resembled some of the athletic figures who may be seen at the side of a north-country wrestling-ring. Indeed, I fancy that Fawcett may have inherited from his father some of the characteristics of the true long-legged, long-limbed Dandie Dinmont type of north-countryman. The impression was, no doubt, fixed in my mental camera because I was soon afterwards surprised by seeing my supposed rustic dining in our College Hall. I insist upon this because it may indicate Fawcett's superficial characteristics on his first appearance at Cambridge.

'Many qualities, which all his friends came to recognise sooner or later, were for the present rather latent, or, maybe, undeveloped. The first glance revealed the stalwart, bucolic figure, with features stamped by intelligence, but that kind of intelligence which we should rather call shrewdness than by any higher name.'

Sports and Games.

At first the men of his own year were inclined to estimate Harry as an outsider in sports and games. His simple provincial ways gave little sign of expert skill. But he won his way in dramatic fashion. An undergraduate nick-named the 'Captain' challenged him to a game of quoits. Salisbury's native game is quoits; Harry was well trained, and won easily. Then the battle shifted to billiards. Captain's score pushed steadily ahead until in a game of a hundred points he had ninety-six to Harry's seventy-five: four points more for the Captain, twenty-five for Harry. The onlookers vociferously offered ten to one on the Captain. Fawcett gravely took all the bets offered at this rate, and any others that he could get, and then calmly, in a single break, made the twenty-five necessary points.

A successful Game of Billiards.

Fawcett is quoted as having given this account, 'Bets were forced on me; but the odds were really more than ten to one against my making twenty-five in any position of the balls, but I saw a stroke which I knew that I could make, and which would leave me a fine game.' No matter by what magic the feat was achieved, it filled his pockets, and cleared for ever any doubts in his companions' minds as to the capacity and shrewdness of 'Old Serpent,' as he was then dubbed, and by which nickname he went for a brief time.

He never gambled again. The story is paralleled in later years by an equally solitary financial speculation. He then showed the same quickness in seizing the facts and calculating the chances, the same boldness in acting on his own judgment, and the same restraint in not repeating the adventure.

He disapproved of gambling, and had a wholesome dislike of it. His sense of fun made it impossible for him ever to have a holier-than-thou attitude, but his common sense and natural goodness kept him singularly free from the failings so common among his associates. While anything but a Puritan, he 'was in all senses perfectly blameless in his life.'

Making Friends.

He had a rare talent for friendship, attracting people to him as easily as he was attracted to them, and his faculty of making friends and keeping them held to the end. He was never known to lose a friend.

Those who knew him well appreciated his strong intellectual equipment. Perhaps his chief characteristics were his absolute normality, his remarkable freedom from self-consciousness, his common sense, and his ever-present sense of fun. These early years at the university, when the lank boy was emerging into the statesman, were years of great happiness and joviality. Fawcett found many congenial spirits, and formed intimacies among men destined to distinguished careers. Most of his associates were good workers, but not particularly given to intellectual subtleties. Music made slight appeal to him, and he was flagrantly ignorant of classics and modern languages, and made no pretence to culture. The young Cambridge men of this period were greatly afraid of sentimentality, and devotees of the 'God of Things as they are.'

But there was one subject peculiarly attractive to the men with whom Fawcett consorted—political economy. And in those days political economy meant Mill. His book, gathering together all the last words of the science, had been written a very few years before Fawcett went to Cambridge. It had had a phenomenal success, and it and its author were enjoying a phenomenal authority. Edward Wilson, a brilliant Senior, well represented the feeling of his day, when he would confute all opposition by an apt quotation, leaving Mill triumphantly supreme, and then close his vindication with the cry, 'Read Mill! Read Mill!' Fawcett did, from early till late, until he knew the book by heart. As he was thoroughly inoculated with this cult, his reverence for Mill was one of his strong steadfast beliefs through life.

Fawcett begrudged time taken from his books, and never rowed in his college boat, although Sir Leslie Stephen writes:

Boating.

'That he occasionally performed in the second boat, I remember by this circumstance, that I can still hear him proclaiming in stentorian tones and in good vernacular from an attic window to a captain of the boat on the opposite side of the quadrangle, and consequently to all bystanders below, that he had a pain in his inside and must decline to row. I have some reason to think that he had felt bad effects from some previous exertions, and had been warned by a doctor against straining himself. I have an impression that there was some weakness in the heart's action. Fawcett, like many men who enjoy unbroken health, was a little nervous about any trifling symptoms. One day we found him lying in bed, complaining lustily of his sufferings, and stating that he had dispatched a messenger to bring him at once the first doctor attainable. A doctor arrived, and his first question as to the nature of Fawcett's last dinner resolved the consultation into a general explosion of laughter, in which the patient joined most heartily.'

It was characteristic of Fawcett that he treated all men as equals, and took from them the best of what they had to offer. He became intimate with men of all ages. Mr. Hopkins, a Peterhouse man, with whom Fawcett read, had received his B.A. in 1827, twenty-five years before Fawcett's appearance at Cambridge; but this difference in age did not prevent a close bond. Fawcett never alluded to Hopkins without great enthusiasm, and in the days of his grave trial this friend was the most helpful of all. He was of great service in the first years at Cambridge, urging Fawcett to regard the mathematical studies necessary for taking a good degree as valuable intellectual gymnastics. Fawcett with his usual keenness and common sense was quite alive to the fact that a good degree was a distinct commercial asset, and said that he would rather be Senior Wrangler in the worst year than second to Sir Isaac Newton. His definite aim in life—a political career—made any wanderings into study for its own sake of no interest to him. He planned through life so to select that he might obtain.

From the days of declaiming in the chalk-pit at Queenwood, Fawcett had realised the value of public speaking.

The Debater.

The great Macaulay, Sir William Harcourt, and other distinguished men had tried their oratorical pinions in flights at the Debating Club called 'The Union.' Fawcett joined, and after some tentative efforts, despite his friends' amusement and discouragement, boldly won his way, and became a good speaker. He worked over his orations carefully, and by great persistence gained an easy and fearless manner of speaking, and we find that he opened debates on National Education and University Reform.

In these years the events which led to the Crimean War provided the chief subjects of debate, such as the foreign policy of Austria and Prussia, the independence of Poland, and the character of the Emperor Nicholas. On these questions Fawcett did not share the views of John Bright, who was then making his great speeches on behalf of peace; but the undergraduate's democratic sympathies are clearly shown in his advocacy of non-sectarian National Education, of a motion that 'the party called "Cobdenites" have done the country good service,' or in favour of a 'considerable extension of the franchise,' and of 'University Reform.'

Good-bye to Grand-iloquence.

It was during this period of careful self-training that Fawcett gradually reduced his style of speaking to that simplicity and directness which became so marked throughout his career. There is a lingering trace of grandiloquence and schoolboy rhetoric in an essay written on the merit of Pope's poetry, but that seems to have been his swan-song to elocution with frills.

The Friend of Friends.

Fawcett left Peterhouse in his second year, and went to Trinity Hall as a pensioner, thus reducing the expense to his father. There chances for scholarship were alluring, and several immigrants from other colleges joined forces at Trinity Hall. There also he met Leslie Stephen, his lifelong friend and biographer, who speaks of this friendship as 'one of the greatest privileges of my life.'

Fawcett set to work with a will to carry off the Senior Wranglership. We are told that in the Tripos, for the first and the last time in his life, Fawcett's nerve failed. Though he got out of bed and ran round the college quadrangle to exhaust himself, he could not sleep, and failed to gain the success which meant so much to him. He sank to seventh; but in spite of his comparative failure he had shown marked ability, and made so great an impression by his work, that he was elected to a fellowship at Christmas 1856.

Pounds and Pence.

He adhered to his boyish ambition of entering Parliament, but there were still great obstacles in his way. Beyond his fellowship, which brought him £250 a year, he had no income of his own. His father was not a rich man, and the strain on his purse to support his other three children was sufficient. Harry resolved, therefore, to make his way by a career at the Bar, and while still at Cambridge entered Lincoln's Inn. When he had won his fellowship he settled in London, and set himself to study law. No one who came in contact with him at this time had any doubt that he would arrive at his goal by main force. A friendly firm of solicitors had already promised that he should have opportunities, and his great talent for working well with all sorts of people, his genius for friendship, and his real business ability bid well for the success of his plan. His will was inflexible, his good-nature chronic, and his acuteness of mind and general ability far beyond the average.

In the mimic legislature of the Westminster Debating Society, which consisted of young barristers and journalists, Fawcett soon became the leader of the Radical party. The organisation followed the form of the House of Commons. It is said that Bulwer Lytton had once paid it a visit, and said afterwards that he had entered in a fit of abstraction, mistaking it for the House of Commons, and only discovered his error upon finding that there were no dull speeches and no one asleep, which seems to prove that it must have been a most remarkable society.

One of his contemporaries, who saw Fawcett in the height of these pseudo-Parliamentary triumphs, speaks of his 'resonant voice, wild hair, and expressive eyes.' But just at this point, when he seemed to be setting with full sail on the channel towards success, his eyes began to trouble him.

CHAPTER IV

A SET BACK

A Trip to France—Wiltshire French—A Discouragement.

In 1857 the great Critchett warned him against making any exertion, and forbade his reading. Though he appeared cheerful as usual with his family, a friend recalls that during his entire career he had never known him to be so depressed.

In 1857 he was glad to find occupation by taking a pupil to Paris. Miss Fawcett went with them. The pupil was to read mathematics and to learn French, while it was hoped that the master's eyes might benefit under the care of foreign specialists, as well as by the change.

The oculists gave him some slight encouragement: one ordered low living, and the other high. It was characteristic of Fawcett that he frugally chose the former.

The Ways of the French.

In Paris our long Wiltshire man seems to have been much of a fish out of water. The Latin morals and customs were naturally not sympathetic to his uncompromising though uncensorious nature. He could never cope successfully with a foreign language. There was even a frequent strong Wiltshire flavour about his English speech. The difference between 'February' and 'Febuwerry' never became apparent to him. At Alderbury he had learnt French with a pronounced English accent. In Paris he now delighted the French ladies at the pension where he stayed with his peculiar and unique speech. There was a Madame Palliasse there whom, much to her joy, he called Madame Peleas.

He came back from France with his eyes still in bad shape and his spirit totally unresponsive to the lure of Gaul.

On his return he was extremely tried by his inability to work. His real feelings about life at this time are well expressed in a letter to his dear friend, Mrs Hodding:

Confession.

'I regard you with such true affection that I have long wished to impart my mind on many subjects.... You know somewhat of my character; you shall now hear my views as to my future. I started life as a boy with the ambition some day to enter the House of Commons. Every effort, every endeavour, which I have ever put forth has had this object in view. I have continually tried, and shall, I trust, still try not only honourably to gratify my desire, but to fit myself for such an important trust. And now the realisation of these hopes has become something even more than the gratification of ambition. I feel that I ought to make any sacrifice, to endure any amount of labour, to obtain this position, because every day I become more deeply impressed with the powerful conviction that this is the position in which I could be of the greatest use to my fellow-men, and that I could in the House of Commons exert an influence in removing the social evils of our country, and especially the paramount one—the mental degradation of millions.

'I have tried myself severely, but in vain, to discover whether this desire has not some worldly source. I could therefore never be happy unless I was to do everything to secure and fit myself for this position. For I should be racked with remorse through life if any selfishness checked such efforts. For I must regard it as a high privilege from God if I have such aspirations, and if He has endowed me with powers which will enable me to assist in such a work.'

This is an interesting revelation of a pure ambition. Fawcett wished to succeed for no self-regarding purpose. His ideals were noble, and his ambition their legitimate accompaniment.

About this time he shows a lively interest in the social condition of the people. After an expedition to some manufacturing towns he mentions an investigation of 'gaols and ragged schools,' and shows much interest in these sombre centres. He describes a meeting with a good gentleman whom he characterises as 'so fine and perfect an example of a venerable Christian.'

Palmerston, Disraeli, and Gladstone.

Even twelve hours spent in one day at the House of Commons does not seem to have been for him an overdose of politics. It did not tax his eyes, and it delighted his ears, though he writes, 'No one need fear obtaining a position in the House of Commons now; for I should say never was good speaking more required. There is not a man in the Ministry can speak but Lord Palmerston; Disraeli is the support of the Opposition; but, although he was considered to have achieved a success that night, it was done by uttering a multitude of words and indulging in a great deal of clap-trap.

'Gladstone made the speech of the evening, and he is a fine speaker. He never hesitates, and his manner and elocution are admirable; in fact, in this he resembles Bright, but is, in my opinion, inferior to Bright, in not condensing his matter.'

Towards the close of this letter there is an exceedingly interesting statement, prophetic of his future interests. He says that he feels that Australia must have in future a great effect on England, and adds these significant words, 'India too is the land I much desire to see and know; and it ought to be by any one who takes part in public life.'

The doctor now forbade Fawcett all reading, for fear that he might lose his sight. He took this sentence philosophically, commenting that it came at an extremely favourable time, when he could best afford to take a holiday. He writes, 'I cannot be sufficiently thankful that it has occurred just now, when perhaps I can spare the time with so little inconvenience.... Maria will resign her needle with great composure to devote herself to reading to me. I shall thus get quite as much reading as I desire, and I can well foresee that, far from being a misfortune, it may become an advantage, since it will perhaps for the next year induce me to *think* more than young men are apt to do: it will give me an opportunity to solidify and arrange my knowledge, and *you* will know how happy Maria and I shall be together.'

Discouraged.

About this time a classmate writes of him: 'We recognised as fully as at a later period his energy and keen intelligence. If we were still a little blind to some of his nobler qualities, we at least recognised in him the thoroughly good fellow, whose success would be as gratifying to his friends as it was confidently anticipated.'

Yes, anticipated and ardently hoped for; but could it be expected by Fawcett himself, doomed as he was to idleness by the condition of his eyes, his doctor's warnings, and their orders for absolute rest—and unfitted as he now was for work, and able only to send an occasional letter to the papers on matters of current interest?

He was staying at his father's house at Longford with such patience as he could muster. He, however, enjoyed sitting in the fields near Salisbury and listening to the sounds about him. The murmuring streams, the songs of birds, and the hum of drowsy insects seemed to bring him comfort and rest.

WINNING BACK

'If you can meet with triumph and disaster
And treat those two impostors just the same.'

KIPLING.

'Life is sweet, brother.'

. . . . . .

'In sickness, Jasper?'
'There's the sun and the stars, brother.'
'In blindness, Jasper?'
'There's the wind on the heath.'

BORROW.

CHAPTER V

DARKNESS

A Shooting Accident — Blindness — Readjustment.

A Shooting Accident.

Unfortunate as was the fate which condemned him to so much trouble with his eyes, it was a fortunate and strange preparation for what was to follow. Obedient to his physician's injunctions to give up work, Fawcett remained with his family near Salisbury. On 15 September 1858, he went shooting with his father. Together they climbed Harnham Hill. Fawcett turned to look back at the glorious view, bathed in an autumn light, the trees, already turning to gold, the village nestled in the valley through which the river Avon wound, the spire of the great cathedral touched with glory by the setting sun. To Fawcett this was one of the loveliest views in England: he looked on all this beauty for the last time.

As they were crossing a field he advanced in front of his father, who, suffering from incipient cataract of the eye, did not see his son. A partridge rose and the father fired, hitting the bird, but some of the stray shot penetrated both the son's eyes, blinding him instantly. To protect his eyes from the glare he was wearing tinted spectacles, both glasses were pierced, but the resistance which they offered to the shot prevented the charge entering the brain, and so probably saved his life. His first thought on being blinded was that he would never again see the beautiful view which he loved so dearly. There is a widely current story, which, however, we have been unable to verify, that after the accident his first words to his agonised father were, 'This shall make no difference.'

Unflinching Bravery.

He was taken back to his father's house in a cart, and his first words to his sister as she received him there were, 'Maria, will you read the newspaper to me?' This way of taking his calamity sounded the key-note of his heroic acceptance of it from the first. His unflinching bravery gave the cue which he wished his family to follow. His calmness remained unaltered even when the doctors gave little encouragement. All knew that there was not much hope, though he was in such splendid physical condition that he suffered very little pain.

Mrs. Fawcett, whom her relations called 'the brightness of the house,' was having tea with some friends when her wounded son was brought in. When she saw him she bravely tried to control her grief, but it was so overwhelming that she took refuge in another room, and only appeared in the short intervals when she was able to master her distress.

In this crisis his sister Maria was a tower of strength. The poor father seemed more sorely stricken by the accident than the son. But for his daughter's wisdom, he would probably have lost his reason. All through the night Maria kept him busy at small, useful tasks, and for several days occupied both her mother and him as fully as possible.

Blindness.

After a lapse of six weeks Fawcett was able for three days to perceive light, but after that the curtain fell for the rest of his life, and he remained in total darkness. In the following June he suffered some pain in one of his eyes, and later submitted to an operation which was unsuccessful, and put the final seal on his calamity. Perhaps the father deserves as much sympathy as the son. Their relations had been particularly affectionate, and were, if possible, more intensely so after the catastrophe. The elder Fawcett often said that his grief at having blinded Henry would be less, if 'the boy' would only complain. But this was perhaps the only way in his life that the son refused to gratify the parent whom he loved so tenderly. He was never known to complain of his loss of sight, and used to say that blindness was not a tragedy, but an inconvenience.

The life-long ambition of Fawcett to lend a hand in public affairs had been shared by his father, and the hope and pride which he felt in his son's career added, if possible, to the tragedy of seeing it so suddenly broken. The indomitable pluck shown by more than one blind man which makes out of his stumbling-block a mounting-stone had yet to be proven. It did not then seem possible for him to win even greater triumphs than he might have won if he had not been forced to sharpen his courage because he had to fight his battle in the dark.

A friend who visited Fawcett a few weeks after the accident found him serene and cheerful, although his father was evidently heart-broken, and his appearance gave abundant evidence of it. Fawcett, though not much given to quotation, was fond at this time of repeating the phrase of Henry V. at the battle of Agincourt:

> 'There is some soul of goodness in things evil,
> Would men observingly distil it out.'

What Fawcett distilled from the evil thing which had befallen him was an iron determination, which triumphed over odds such as few have encountered on any battlefield.

A Cloud.

But the blind man's horizon had not yet cleared. His outlook, despite the loving care of his family, was still sad, and though he gave no sign, there was a fearful slough of despond still to be struggled through. Ten minutes after the accident, he had made up his mind to stick to his pursuits as much as possible, but how nearly possible was it for a blind man to succeed in Parliament, and to give a helpful impetus to the affairs of nations? This was still at Fawcett's time in England untested and remained for him to show. He lacked fortune and social position to clear the road for him, and the letters of condolence that poured in mostly obstructed his path with futile sentimentality. He said, 'they give more pain than comfort,' and added that nothing pained him so much as these letters. The writers counselled resignation to the will of Providence, meekness, submission, and of course all implied inaction. But Fawcett asked what was the will of Providence. Why, without trying, should he suppose that inaction would be the nobler part for him to play. His sister read to him all the missives from the Job's comforters, and he, though much saddened, listened, 'in a fixed state of stoical calm.'

The Message of a Friend.

Into this atmosphere, heavy with grief, came the message of a friend. His dear old Cambridge teacher, Hopkins, wrote admitting that blindness is 'one of the severest bodily calamities that can befal us,' yet added cheerfully: 'But depend upon it, my dear fellow, it must be our own fault if such things are without their alleviation.... Give up your mind to meet the evil in the worst form it can hereafter assume. Now it seems to me that your mind is eminently adapted to many of those studies which may be followed with least disadvantage without the help of sight....

'I would suggest your directing your attention to subjects of a philosophical and speculative character, such as any branch of mental science and the history of its progress; the Philosophy of Physical Science, as Herschel's work in *Lardner's Encyclopædia*, Whewell's *Inductive Philosophy*, etc., or any work treating on the general principles, views, and results of physical science. Political Economy, statistics, and social science in general are assuming interesting forms in the present day.

'What a wide range of speculative study, full of interest, do these subjects present to us! For any part of which, if I mistake not, your mind is well qualified.

'The evil that has fallen upon you, like all other evils, will lose half its terror if regarded steadfastly in the face with the determination to subdue it as far as it may be possible to do so.

'Cultivate your intellectual resources (how thankful you may be for them!) and cultivate them systematically: they will avail you much in your many hours of trial. Under any circumstances I hope you will visit Cambridge from time to time. I'll lend you my aid to amuse you by talking philosophy or reading an act of Shakespeare or a canto from Byron. I shall certainly avail myself of the first opportunity I have of paying you a visit at Longford, and shall engage you for my guide across the chalk hills. I may then perhaps find the means of indoctrinating you with a few healthy geological principles.'

Hopkins had struck the right chord. He roused his pupil from his depression and gave him new hope and ambition. 'Keep that letter for me,' he said to his sister, and from its arrival dated his returning zeal and the spontaneous cheerfulness which heretofore had been so skilfully assumed.

A Rigid Resolution.

Though the sanity and wisdom of this letter aroused Fawcett as nothing had before, it is not to be understood that his taking up life again depended upon the spur given to his hope and self-confidence by his old friend, but this did come at the psychological moment. It enabled him to shoulder his burden with more courage, and to begin again climbing towards the ambitions he had entertained before his blindness. Unhelped he had planned to travel the road already begun, deviating as little as possible from the course before mapped out; and he would have done so without the comfort from his friend's advice. But the letter was undoubtedly a first milestone on his race towards the goal which he had set himself.

Much has been said of the philosophy which is apt to accompany blindness, of the resignation and calm of those afflicted with it. The unusual feature in the bravery with which Fawcett met his calamity was his almost instantaneous resolution to disregard it, and to make good just as he would have made good without it. Too much honour cannot be given him for this extraordinary and immediate courage.

Very soon after the accident he took up walking, and at once showed his fearlessness while going between his brother and a friend who has recorded the brave adventure.

Walking.

On leaving the house, he struck out at once with the long, quick strides of his old walking era, and naturally stumbled almost at the first step. One of the party caught him by the arm, and begged him to pick his steps more carefully. 'Leave me alone!' was his reply; 'I've got to learn to walk without seeing, and I mean to begin at once—only tell me when I am going off the road.' To say that he knew not fear would be to give an impression of callousness which would be entirely false; but it can be truly said that fear never kept him from carrying out his purpose.

An early glimpse of the hard conflict and longing of his soul was given when walking with his dearly loved sister. He turned to her suddenly as if he had been thinking, and asked if she knew Southey's 'Hymn before Sunrise in the Valley of Chamounix.' When she replied that she did not, he astonished her by reciting the poem with rare beauty and fervour. The vibrant voice gathered intensity as, with that wistful expression so often on his newly blinded face, he repeated the last lines:

> 'Rise, O ever rise!
> Rise like a cloud of incense from the Earth!
> Thou kingly Spirit throned among the hills,
> Thou dread ambassador from Earth to Heaven,
> Great Hierarch! tell thou the silent sky,
> And tell the stars, and tell yon rising sun,
> Earth, with her thousand voices, praises God.'

MISS MARIA FAWCETT

Social Ways.

After his accident Fawcett took his meals with his sister from a tray in the drawing-room. When some weeks had passed, he was persuaded to venture out with her to a quiet supper at the home of friends. Finding that it was not a for-midable undertaking after all, and that he had an extremely interesting time, he determined to see as much of people as possible, and resumed his social ways.

It was inevitable that at first his merriment and cheerfulness were a little bit laboured, but in an astonishingly short time they became invariable, and those closest to him detected no permanent depression. About everything but his sadness under his affliction, Fawcett was frank, but about this sadness he remained bravely reticent.

He soon began candidly to enjoy life, and he seems to have gotten infinitely more of its beauty and happiness than the average person who is without handicaps. He had only had one fear, which he confided to his sister: it would be unbearable for him if through loss of physical force he should become useless.

Despite very great difficulty, Fawcett for some time tried to keep up writing with his own hand, and there are still several of his autograph letters. But he found the effort so great that he soon gave it up and depended entirely on dictation. He was not entirely loath to do this, because he thought the practice of dictation useful to him as a speaker. He never mastered Braille or any other system of printing for the blind, but depended on being read to.

Catalogued Collars.

In many minor things Fawcett never acquired the dexterity possible to those who are blinded in youth. When his catastrophe came his habits were already too fixed, and he was too mature to adapt himself readily in unimportant matters. But his ingenuity in studying out scientific management of all the little problems of daily routine was marvellously practical and at times even comic. For example, he had all his clothes carefully and legibly labelled with numbers, placed so as not to show during wear. In this way his garments might easily be identified by any one not familiar with his wardrobe. If he came home in a great hurry to metamorphise his attire, directions like the following to his family or an aide-de-camp were not infrequent. He would call in his clarion, cheerful voice, probably from the door as he entered: 'I must dress quickly. Please help. Coat one, vest six, collar one, trousers three; shoes and socks twelve and thirteen.' The rest we will leave to imagination, but there was no detail, even to pocket-handkerchiefs, which did not have its allotted place and catalogue number.

A Hero to his Tailor.

He seems long to have remained faithful to his Salisbury tailor, a charming person of the old school who recently vouchsafed to the author the following recollections of his distinguished client: 'Mr. Fawcett was very matter of fact and methodical. A very honest kind of man, a sterling man. He was very susceptible to cold, and was apt to carry changes of different underwear with him. He was particular about the material which he bought for his clothes, and always felt of it. He wouldn't be humbugged. You couldn't help liking him. He was that loose and easy in his walk, his limbs didn't seem to belong to him. I often heard him at the hustings, he spoke to the point—he made a thorough impression.'

CHAPTER VI

HAPPINESS

The Clear-sighted Man—A Scot's Accent—Mountain Climbing—
Skating—Riding, etc.

His friends all testify to his spirit, his normal view of life frequently making them forget the fact of his blindness. A distinguished writer and diplomat, who had known Fawcett, on being asked what impression had been produced on him, replied quickly and quite simply, 'I think that he was an extraordinarily clear-sighted man.' Stephen in his biography uses this sentence: 'Fawcett had come to *see* more distinctly the real tendency of the proposal and to feel the full force of the objections to which he had never been blind.' Such remarks illustrate Fawcett's power of making people utterly forget his blindness.

How to be happy.

He was always grateful when his companions paid no attention to his affliction, and would talk to him about the scenery which they passed and the people whom they met as if he too could see them. He kept his resolve to be as happy as was possible, and often said: 'There is only one thing that I ever regret, and that is to have missed a chance for enjoyment.' He told his friends that he intended to live to be ninety, and to relish every day of his life. He deliberately set about cultivating those tastes which would redound to his happiness: he taught himself to smoke, he patiently learned to listen to music, which had never unfolded its full joys to him before he had lost his sight. He so far succeeded as to be able to enjoy concerts and the opera.

Doubtless, he systematically trained himself to remember. It was often remarked of him that if he had heard a voice once he would remember it again years after. One day in the Cambridge streets he was accosted by a Scottish professor. Fawcett could not remember him, but encouraged him to talk, and kept up his end of a long conversation. After a good twenty minutes, a trick in the Scot's accent betrayed him, and Fawcett enthusiastically grasped his hand, and said, 'How do you do, Clerk Maxwell?'

He never attempted to modify his vocabulary to fit his infirmity, and though the effect was at times strange he would greet people in the most natural way in the world with: 'How do you do? how well you're looking'; or 'What's the matter, you're looking pale to-day? Too much work, eh?' He commented on a friend's looking old, and added: 'But when men with that colour hair turn grey, they do look prematurely old.'

It was not unusual for him to mimic people, whom he had only known since his blindness, reproducing their gestures as well as their speech.

Games.

Later he learned to play cribbage and écarté with cards pricked by his secretary with raised dots, in the fashion used by the blind to produce tactile prints. It took him but three days to conquer all difficulties in this new system, and he played with quickness and enjoyment. It is of no small interest to those who have studied the psychology of those blinded by accident in maturity to note this successful development of card playing. Shortly after his accident he had made an attempt which proved a total failure and yet afterwards he took it up without effort. This point should be dwelt on, and may well give courage to many an adult who is blinded. It shows that it is worth while to repeat often, and to hope for success in experiments which have been abandoned as futile.

His hearing developed great acuteness, so that he could tell in towns by the pressure of the atmosphere if he was passing an opening caused by a cross street. When he walked in the country he loved the sound of the leaves, the feel of grass, the springing of the sod beneath his feet, the note of a bird or the leap of a fish. He seems to have tried to gather from his friends' descriptions an even deeper insight into the charm and subtleties of Nature than before it was shut out from his bodily vision. When, later, he enjoyed driving, he would stop the carriage in order to see the view at some favourite point. He was so fond of the view at Brighton that he often telegraphed a friend there to take him a walk to Rottingdean. He always enjoyed this intensely, and spoke of the exquisite prospect as of one of the most wonderful in England. A breath of the sea stimulated him greatly. After a storm he loved to listen to the booming and breaking of the waves on the shore, and to feel the burn of the brine which was cast in his face as he breasted the receding gale. The little shells and the seaweed interested him, and he liked to pass the latter between his fingers to get the slippery gluey feeling, and to play with their little pods and queer tentacles.

Enjoying the View from the Mountain Tops.

Fawcett loved great heights and mountains, a fellow climber says: 'I went up Helvellyn with Fawcett. It was his first mountain since he was blind—by no means his last. He held one end of a stick and I the other, to direct his turns; and that was all the aid he needed. But it warmed one's heart to see his hearty enjoyment. He would have all the views described to him, what hills and lakes he saw, what colours they were, where the mist floated, and he anxiously asked of his secretary who was with us whether he enjoyed it as much as he expected.'

Later he climbed the Cima di Jazzi, in order to see the glorious array of snow-covered peaks. It does not seem too much to believe that the highly developed blind have a feeling of the beauty which we say they cannot see, and a realisation of its presence which we lack and which it is impossible for them to explain.

Though science has not yet been able to classify this faculty it may before long, and in the meantime there is sufficient evidence that this unclassified vision of the sightless to a great extent illumines their darkness.

Excepting cricket and rackets, he gave up none of the sports of which he was already fond.

The Giant's Stride.

All his friends are agreed that it was almost impossible to keep up with him in his walks. They tried to modify his break-neck pace by various devices, such as engaging him in absorbing discussions, or stopping to talk to some one on the road. But in vain. His long legs would shoot out like relentless walking beams, and if his friend happened to be small and holding on to Fawcett's arm before long he would be swept off his feet, hanging on like a mere appendage to the rushing blind man.

Fawcett's recollection for the places that he had known before his blindness was astonishing. He could even remember in closest detail the country where he had been as a child at school.

Skating.

Having before his accident been a powerful skater he now took it up again, and after a few strokes showed no hesitancy. He was known even to accompany a skating race, leaving the course clear for the competitors and himself unaccompanied getting over the rough ice on the side. Of his first attempt we read:

'After a few strokes the only difficulty was to keep his pace down to mine. We each held one end of a stick, and as we were on the crowded Serpentine, we came into a good many collisions. As, however, we were a couple, and one of us a heavy man, we had decidedly the best of these encounters, especially as the conscience of our antagonists was on our side when they saw that they had tripped up a blind man.'

In after years his recklessness became proverbial. He had been on a long expedition on the frozen Cam one cold winter, and was returning at sunset, chatting gaily with his friends to the accompanying click of their skates. They were flying along at a good fifteen miles an hour when they came upon a treacherous stretch of very rough ice. Fawcett, who accepted ice baths as part of the fun, urged them forward, zealously calling out: 'Go on—I only got my legs through!'

Riding.

In the early stages of his blindness, Fawcett's purse did not permit him to ride much. Moreover, some narrow escapes from accident—he was at one time nearly crushed at Salisbury by a cart—made him for a short time hesitate as to its expediency. But later he took it up with enthusiasm, at first accompanied by a riding master, and later by groups of friends. One of these tells how he would often ride over to Newmarket to spend Sunday. During the Sabbath he would nearly walk his friend off his legs, and on other days contented himself with walking his horse off its legs. With a box of sandwiches provided for luncheon, Fawcett would ride over from Cambridge at Christmas time to feast on the sunny side of the Devil's Ditch. He loved the chalk downs, and often stopped at a cottage to ask for a draught of the sparkling, deep-well water. He enjoyed, too, gossiping with the shepherds about the flocks, for his early interest in agricultural matters was through life a marked characteristic. Once he came across the harriers, and joined in their gallops, trusting entirely to the prudence of his horse to select the most favourable gaps in the hedgerows.

A frequent companion on these rides tells how one day, going at a brisk pace, she was so interested in something he was telling her that she did not see until within a few feet of it that they were at the edge of a precipitous gravel pit. Fearing to alarm Fawcett she simply called out, 'stop at once, please.' Fawcett, always quick to act, pulled up short, and but for his prompt response to her call would certainly have been killed. Fawcett was so reckless and enthusiastic an equestrian that it is still a well-remembered tradition in the livery-stables at Cambridge that Professor Fawcett took so much vitality out of his mounts that he was always charged extra. It must not be gathered that he was inhuman to his horses—they probably had just as good a time, relatively, as he had, but whatever he did, he did in a whole-souled and muscular fashion.

Fishing.

But for Fawcett, who had been trained from childhood as a fisherman, the crowning joy of all sports was a good fishing expedition. Very soon after the accident, he took up his fishing again. He remembered his native stream well, and to the end of his life he was always eager to run down to Salisbury to fish. His letters to his father abound in reference to angling parties, past and to come. He gave directions about his fishing-boots (they were so frequently in use that they must have had a simple number in his catalogue of clothes) and instructions to secure some expert angler to accompany him, or framed some subtle tactics for way-laying and ensnaring some particularly elusive aquatic prey, who had perhaps been known to his neighbours but had remained uncaught by them.

Trout and Political Economy.

Many friends urged him to try their waters for trout, pike, salmon, jack-fishing, and he enjoyed their hospitality greatly. His father who was devoted to the sport, in which he excelled even after his ninetieth year, was very fond of accompanying him. Fawcett's early practice enabled him to throw a fly with great accuracy. He was fond of combining his amusements, and would wade in the stream while one of his great friends often went with him, though walking on the bank so as not to throw his shadow on the water, but so that he could talk to his heart's content without disturbing the angler. Fawcett was wont to say that trout hear very badly, and are not distracted by political economy. So fond was Fawcett of the study of his favourite subject that his first secretary records how in moments snatched between fishing he would accompany Fawcett to a tea-house, where he would read to him Mill's *Political Economy*.

Those who accompanied him fishing are agreed that he was a much better fisherman than sighted people generally are. This may have been due to his extraordinary patience, or to his zeal in learning from the experts with whom he associated.

A Salisbury friend who often fished with him says: 'He would make his way through anything. He often walked along the river's edge fishing, and he never fell in. One day he was fishing and caught his line in a tree overhead. He exclaimed to his secretary, who came up, "Can't you see it?" then, with added impatience, "See it's up there, I can see it!"'

With his characteristic pluck he did not hesitate to wade in the stream or to cross a narrow plank. He enjoyed all the roughing incidents in fishing, even bumping about in a donkey cart full of fish, and he was particularly glad to meet the country folk and have a chat with them.

CHAPTER VII

DISTRACTION

Fishing—In the Commons—Need for Distraction—What Helen Keller
thinks—Sir Francis Campbell—Leap Frog—Despair and Cheer—
Paupers and Political Economy.

What Fishing meant for Fawcett.

It sometimes seems inconsistent that one so acutely sensitive as Fawcett was
to suffering of all kinds should not have hesitated to get pleasure from a sport involving the necessary cruelty of fishing. In discussing this, Fawcett at times would
maintain the usual ground of the fishes insensibility to pain, but again he would
frankly justify it as the best method of keeping himself employed and distracted
from the weighty problems which often overburdened him.

It must not be forgotten that, however clever in adapting themselves to their
misfortune the blind are, they are relieved from the thousands of the distractions
which disturb the concentration of even the best seeing worker. In his lecture-room
the sighted teacher is unconsciously drawn from the monotony of his one purpose
by seeing his mind play on the sensibilities of his hearers.

Screened Bobbing Bonnets.

In the House of Commons the statesman's mind is unconsciously diverted
by the lights, the expressions of his opponents, the sympathy on the faces of his
partisans, the guests in the gallery, to say nothing of his imaginings concerning
those hidden and gracious unseen personalities behind the screen in the ladies'
gallery—that screen which, perhaps more than anything else in the House of
Commons, piques the curiosity of the beholder, and sets his thoughts aglow with
the mysteries of the Orient. If the indiscreet and objectionable person who devised
that screen had left the wives and mothers and sweethearts of the members to
regale the combatants in the arena beneath them with a smile of approbation, or
a glimpse of their spring bonnets, or even the pang caused by the thought of the
inevitable bill which belongs to such plumage, the path of duty and politics would
have been less dull.

Then, think of the countless literary distractions, the day's paper, the illustrated magazine, the picture posters, and even the advertisements which to the
hurrying business man unconsciously suggest fresh trains of thought. Again, the
sight of the crowd, with its noble and curious personalities, or the occasional patch

of colour made by the passing omnibus whose garish poster proclaims the latest star at the theatre. All these, and countless others, make up a kaleidoscope, which, however taxing and at times palling to the man with sight, are counter-irritants which make it difficult for him to over-concentrate or to become exhausted by harping continuously on one thought, to the exclusion of all else. To think without interruption the seeing man sometimes closes his eyes. The blind man's eyes are always closed, and therefore to keep his spirits bright, to prevent morbidity and even insanity, occupations and amusement are not only advisable, but imperative. In frank recognition of this Fawcett felt that the larger good—his usefulness to the community—justified his 'going fishing.'

What Helen Keller thinks.

The great need of recreation brings as its corollary the advantages for uninterrupted thought, which are among the alleviations of the loss of sight. Helen Keller, in answer to the question, What is it to be blind? said joyfully, 'To be blind is to see the bright side of life.' She is perfectly sincere in this, and feels that in blindness, uncomeliness and ugliness can never obtrude, while imagination is free to paint the most sublime pictures. Not a few blind people have said that they would prefer not to see, because with sight would come many disillusionments.

It is a question of great interest whether either Miss Keller or Fawcett, without their spur from blindness, without that need of iron determination and unflinching pluck to win their race in the dark, would, as seeing people, have attained their respective distinction and have been such great servants of humanity. Many fail on account of the insurmountable barriers which seem to accompany blindness, but not a few heroic souls are developed and stimulated by their blindness in a way that nothing else could have equalled. To these ranks it seems that Fawcett belonged.

He hesitated greatly to allude to his blindness, and we find him doing so voluntarily, only to help those similarly afflicted. It was a very painful thing for him to speak on behalf of the blind, and on one such occasion he confided to a friend that he had never been so nervous in his life. He hated to be put, or to place himself, in a position to evoke pity, still more to seem to show what he had achieved despite his handicap.

He said to the blind, 'Act as if you were not blind, be of good courage, and help yourselves.' He advised the seeing, 'Do not patronise; treat us without reference to our misfortune; and, above all, help us to be independent.' Also, he emphasised that 'home associations are for the blind as important as for you' (meaning the seeing); 'you must not wall up the blind.' 'Do not sever them from all the pleasures and fascinations of home.'

Sir Francis Campbell.

He was particularly interested in the work of Dr. Campbell, later Sir Francis Campbell, the intrepid American blind man who was knighted by King Edward for the splendid work he had done to emancipate the blind through education.

Fawcett spoke often for the benefit of Campbell's work at the Royal Normal College for the Blind. The following quotations from Fawcett's speeches were written for this book by some of the blind stenographers employed at the college, the work of which was inspired by Sir Francis.

Fawcett, referring to the blind, said, 'Nothing, he found, was so hard to bear as to hear people, when they spoke of the blind, assume a patronising tone towards them, as if they were suffering from something for which in some mysterious way they should feel thankful. The kindest thing that could be done or said to a blind person was not to use patronising language, but to tell him, as far as possible, to be "of good cheer," to give him confidence that help would be afforded him whenever it was required, that there was still good work for him to do, and the more active his career, the more useful his life to others, the more happy his days to himself.'

Fawcett Reminiscences.

To a blind and most responsive audience he said, 'I did not lose my sight until I had reached manhood. I was twenty-five years of age at the time, and when I knew that my sight was gone, never to return, many friends came forward and, prompted by the kindest motives, advised me to adopt a life of quiet contemplation. I very soon, however, came to the resolution to live, as far as possible, just as I had lived before, following the same pursuits and enjoying, as well as I could, the same pleasures. (Cheers.) I would strongly advise those who may be similarly situated to try to pursue the same course, for I have found that there is a wide range of amusements in which I can take just the same delight as I did in days of yore. No one can more enjoy catching a salmon in the Tweed or the Spey, or throwing a fly in some quiet trout stream in Wiltshire or Hampshire. I can take the greatest delight, accompanied by a friend, in a gallop over the turf; a long row from Oxford to London gives me the same invigorating exercise that it used to do, and during the recent long frost I do not think any one in the whole country found more pleasure than I did in a long day's skating with a friend. Often in the Cambridgeshire fens I have skated fifty or sixty miles in the day. (Cheers.) It is a true remark that nature provides a wonderful compensating power, but I am bound to say that of all the compensations which I have found, the greatest is the generous and cordial readiness with which people are ever ready to come forward to offer us that assistance without which we are often powerless to do anything. (Cheers.) This with regard to our lot is certainly a silver lining to the dark cloud.'

'There are at the present time some nine or ten different systems of printing for the blind. Each of these systems has its different advocates, and as the cost of printing is very heavy, a great and unnecessary outlay is incurred in printing the same book in many different ways. If an agreement could be arrived at to adopt one particular system, with the same outlay the numbers of books that would be brought within the reach of the blind would be increased manyfold, and an inestimable boon would be conferred upon them by having brought within their reach a greater number of the masterpieces of English literature.'

Leap-frog.

Fawcett spoke of an apparently hopeless blind boy who had come to the institution. At last his chance of making his way seemed assured, because Dr. Campbell had induced him to play leap-frog. Fawcett said that that seemed to him 'the one test which ought to be applied to any institution devoted to the training of the youthful blind. Notwithstanding,' he said, 'no one felt more than he, or was more anxious to acknowledge, that, however independent they might be made, they still constantly required some assistance; and he felt that whatever he might be doing at the present time, he should be reduced to a state of entire helplessness if it were not for the friendly arm and helping voice which were always extended to him.'

An Apostle of Despair.

At a meeting to promote a scheme for the benefit of the blind an apostle of despair began a prepared speech; but Fawcett, who had preceded him, so completely convinced his audience of the sanity of a cheerful and useful outlook when helping the blind that the apostle of despair found the wind completely taken out of his sails, and was forced to sit down with his speech unfinished. At the end of the controversy, when the gloomy speaker had retired, Fawcett said to Lady Campbell, 'I hope I didn't hit him too hard!'

Fawcett was most generous to his opponents, and feared lest his victories should have caused them the slightest suffering.

When Postmaster-General he was anxious to bring deaf and dumb assorters into the Post Office.

When he heard that telegraphy was thought of as a possible occupation for the blind, he sent for Sir Francis Campbell, to talk the matter over at the Post Office with the Comptroller-General. 'For,' said Fawcett, 'if you think it is practical for the blind to be employed in this way, I shall give them a chance.' The plan was not considered practical, though Fawcett was eager for it.

Heartening the Blind.

He was zealous to do anything he could by his energy and gaiety to help those afflicted as he was but who took a more despondent view of their condition.

The frank recognition which he gives of his dependence in his blindness on the help of others gives touching insight into one of the integral qualities of his friendship. A friendship meant for him the acceptance of countless little services which it would be a privilege for his friend to perform, and while tacitly accepting these aids Fawcett felt deeply thankful, and sought automatically to do what he could in return. His kindness was not in the least of the give-and-take type; he revelled in giving fully of his life and strength where there could not possibly be any return.

Wright of Salisbury.

Paupers and Political Economy.

An old fisherman and a delightful character, Wright of Salisbury, was a great friend of Fawcett. Wright was an ardent politician and a pronounced Liberal; that he was a celebrated angler is proved by Fawcett's remark, 'Why, Wright, I was in Wales fishing and they knew you there, and when I was in Scotland I asked if they knew you, and they said, "Oh yes, quite well."' The two used to go fishing together, and Fawcett would make special request of his companion to tell him of every blind person they met. He never met any one afflicted with blindness without offering help. On one occasion, Wright has chronicled, he was greatly concerned after he had given a poor blind person alms, and asked whether Wright had noticed what coin he had given to the woman. When the fisherman said he thought that it was a 'florin or half a crown,' Fawcett exclaimed with a sigh of relief, 'Oh, I am so glad; I was afraid I gave her a penny.'

His ear was wonderfully acute, and he would detect the tapping of a beggar's stick on the sidewalk at a great distance, or in the midst of the roar of London traffic. The distinguished political economist, as soon as he heard this little progressive noise, would let all his well-assorted theories of economy and social justice fly to the winds and hail the approaching beggar merrily, stop and have a few cheery words with him, and before they parted gave him some pence. His secretary never knew him to overlook a beggar or to fail to give him money. It is the only instance that I can find in his life where he did not live up to his principles.

CAMBRIDGE AGAIN

'And ye shall know the truth, and the truth shall make you free.'
'Be swift to hear; and let thy life be sincere; and with patience
give answer.'

CHAPTER VIII

THE PROBLEM OF THE POOR

A Prime Object—Lincoln—Leslie Stephen—Daily Life at Cambridge—Deepening Interest in Social Questions.

Prime Object of his Career.

When Fawcett first began to pick up the threads of his life again he planned to continue reading for the Bar, and obtained special facilities from the Council of Legal Education. But about a year after his blindness he decided to give up law altogether. There have been successful blind lawyers, but Fawcett's goal was not law but Parliament, and he shrewdly perceived that he might make his way to the front as quickly by distinction as a political economist as by good work at the Bar. To live at Cambridge among the colleges and streets that he knew and loved, and among the many intimate friends he had there, appealed very strongly to him in his first blindness.

He determined to avail himself of all that the University had to give him. While continuing his economic studies he took occasion to give lectures and to attend and speak at meetings of learned societies. Above all, he sought to find and win a constituency.

Personality at twenty-five.

Let us try to realise what manner of man he was when he went back to Trinity Hall. He was a little over twenty-five years of age, and a little over six feet three inches in height, not broad in proportion, but lanky; of commanding presence, he had a voice of such volume that his friends used to say it 'scorned concealment.' Frank and transparent in all his relations with men and women, he hated subterfuge of any kind. His quick kindness saved him from hurting any one's feelings, though he was still somewhat rough in his ways. Never stereotyped in appearance or manner, nor really conventional, he had a distinction quite his own. His pronunciation never became entirely urbane, and his friends had much difficulty in persuading him that Professor Tyndall might be right in saying that glacier ice was a viscous fluid, but that he had never asserted it to be 'vicious.'

Fawcett hated tyranny in every form. His sympathies ranged from the smallest child forced to work in the English mines to the American negro enslaved, whose problems were then beginning to shake the Western Hemisphere. Deeply interested in America, Fawcett became an ardent Federalist and a great admirer of

Lincoln.

English Fun, American Humour.

Not only by his build and love of justice does he suggest the great emancipator for whom he felt such interest. If Lincoln had lived in England it is probable that he would have lent a hand in some of the many problems which Fawcett helped to solve; while if Fawcett had been born in a cabin in Kentucky instead of by Salisbury Plain, it is not unthinkable that he might have been a great fighter for the cause of freedom and integrity of the Union. Another strong characteristic which these men shared was an ever-present sense of humour. In Fawcett it was akin to that of the big schoolboy; practical jokes appealed to him and called forth his ringing laughter. His fun was of a hearty kind that suited his voice and his huge type. Perhaps Fawcett's humour would best be described by the American as an English sense of fun, and by the Englishman as not in the least American.

Lincoln's immortal wit, both in its defects as well as its perfection, could only have been the outcome of American conditions. But for the support and relief afforded to Lincoln by his intense, unfailing humour he would probably not have been able to bear the strain necessary to accomplish his mighty task; but for his present love of fun and his elastic buoyancy of spirit Fawcett would not have been able to master his great affliction and to have continued in his struggle on behalf of the down-trodden, ignorant, and afflicted of his country.

Grey Suits.

His Conservative Salisbury tailor said recently of him, 'He was a very great anti-slavery man, and sympathised with the abolitionists in America.' We can imagine Fawcett holding forth in stentorian tones about the rights of the negro, while his small, gentle tailor tried in vain to make the new grey suit fit his giant customer. By the same authority we learn that Fawcett 'was very partial to grey suits.'

Fawcett and Stephen.

He established himself at the Hall, as the college is known in Cambridge, in rooms in the main court that looked south and gathered all the sun grey Cambridge had to give them. They were on the first floor, and above them his attendant and guide, Brown, occupied some garrets. Leslie Stephen roomed on the same floor, and could reach Fawcett by passing through a lecture-room. The two men were always together, and Stephen writes that Fawcett's rooms seemed part of his own.

Onlookers have said that Stephen's care of Fawcett at this time 'was beautiful to see'; it 'was almost womanly.' The two men were curiously different in temperament and traditions. They seem to have shared little but their earlier politics and their love of walking. Stephen, from whom Meredith is said to have modelled his character of Vernon Whitford, was a writer and student, a descendant of writers and students. Though he seems to have much enjoyed the Cambridge society in which he was then living, he was usually the silent member of a company where

Fawcett dominated by force of energy if not always by the intrinsic value of what he said.

Fawcett's room was gay with photographs and the flowers which the blind man loved to have about him. His fondness for them was a strong and charming trait. In these days he usually wore a flower in his button-hole. He loved having them about him; through their fragrance and the delicacy of their petals he took in their beauty so completely that he seemed to lose little because he could not see them with his bodily eye.

The Fellows' Garden on the Cam.

Trinity Hall is in the very heart of Collegiate Cambridge, wedged in between the Senate House and the Cam. Along the river lies the Fellows' Garden that Henry James has so warmly praised. After Fawcett's death Stephen spoke of this garden and Fawcett's love for it.

'I always associated Fawcett with a garden. He loved a garden because he could there take the exercise in which he delighted without the precautions necessary for a blind man in public places. He loved it because he heartily enjoyed the sweet air and the scent of flowers and the song of birds. He loved it because he could ... enjoy even the sights, the sky and the trees, through the eyes of others. He loved it not least because a garden is the best of all places for those long talks with friends which were among the greatest pleasures of his life. The garden where I oftenest met Fawcett, and where I have talked with him for long hours, never clouded by an unkind word, is the garden of an old Cambridge College with a smooth bowling green, and a terrace walk by the side of the river, and a noble range of old chestnut trees and the grand pinnacles of King's College Chapel looking down through the foliage.'

Within the limits of his college Fawcett moved freely and alone. He would cross the court and find his way up and down stairs quite unattended, verifying places with his cane. A Cambridge friend tells how his coming would be heralded by his well-known step and by the tapping of that same cane. Announcing himself outside the door with 'Hello, are you there?' he would come into the room, waving his stick about to locate objects. A hearty handshake would be followed by some such comment as 'How well you are looking,' or 'I am sorry you are not looking so well to-day,' this information probably reaching him from the greeting of what was to him the tell-tale voice of his host.

Sometimes he would wander in the court at night, annoying the sleepers by his tapping on the stone flags. Was it as a just retribution that one night his sleep was hopelessly broken by the continuous singing of a nightingale near his window? At last he could stand it no longer, and sought for a missile to drive the bird away; his soap proving the only available ammunition, he hurled it at the offending mistrel, and routed him completely. But though the blind man achieved his purpose without injury to the nightingale, later he had a long and futile hunt for his cherished bit of soap, and his lusty voice was heard echoing along the historic Cambridge walls, 'Oh, I say, who will lend me some soap?' until that essential was provided by a neighbour.

He worked in the mornings, and between tea and dinner, the afternoons were given up to exercise, and the evenings to conversations interminable.

Work and Walks.

His favourite walk was over the Gog Magogs, the Cambridge Hills. They are perhaps the lowest hills to be dignified with the name, but he insisted that the air was purer on their summit than anywhere else, because there was practically nothing between him and the Ural Mountains. He would call attention to the outlook towards the distant towers of Ely Cathedral, and invariably paused at certain points 'to look at the view.' Through life he took the keenest joy in walking to some place where the scenery was beautiful, and, helped by his friends' description, he would see with their eyes. His love of Nature was intense; he would often describe a sunset with such vividness that he himself forgot whether he had actually seen it before he was blind, or had only beheld it in his mind's eye.

The fascination political economy had for him grew as he worked. To him it was never the dry and impersonal science which freezes so many enthusiasms, but the science which is necessary knowledge for the statesman who wishes to better the condition of the man furthest down. We have seen how Fawcett's interest in the market folk at Salisbury began when he was a child. The sight of many industrious, hard-working people unable to support themselves in spite of the greatest frugality, and having nothing better to look forward to than the poorhouse, had left an indelible impression; he wanted to free these people so that they might have rational lives with a fair return for their hard work. His father's political example and his own sympathetic nature and wish to serve had made him from his youth a Radical. He had a passion for justice and a zeal to redress wrongs and to liberate the poor from the bondage in which their ignorance kept them. He regarded political economy and kindred studies as means to his end, and Parliament as the ultimate stronghold, from which he could direct his campaign. This was his prime object, and while achieving it he gathered on his way all the happiness and merriment that was honourably to be had.

Freeing the Fellowships.

In the year that Fawcett was elected fellow of his college the question of reforming the tenure of the fellowships was newly opened, and at once he took a hot and revolutionary part. When he returned to Cambridge he continued to uphold a policy which would leave the fellowships open to the freest competition. He insisted that neither religious opinions nor other disabilities, many of which existed, should be any bar. The issues involved by these reforms were intricate and came up for discussion in the House of Commons when Fawcett was a member; but all through their varying phases he kept to the one view that fellowships should be aids to poor men who desired a university training and should be open to the competition of the ablest.

But in 1858 fellowships could be held by unmarried men only. Cambridge society consisted largely of young men before their departure into those wider fields which permit of matrimony, and a few belated seniors lingering behind, bachelors by predilection or compulsion. The youthfulness of the majority appealed to the youthful; sanguine, buoyant, and sociable, they could boast of sufficient ability to have won them places in open competition. If they gave evidence of the truth of the famous admonition of Dr. Thompson, the Master of Trinity College, that 'we are none of us infallible, not even the youngest of us,' their intercourse was only the more lively.

Into this circle Fawcett came like a huge magnet, drawing to himself all kinds of curiously different people. He was most heartily welcomed everywhere, and even when his hot Radicalism encountered in some senior a wall of Conservative opposition, the wall soon crumbled under Fawcett's unquestionable sincerity and good-will.

CHAPTER IX

THE GOOD SAMARITAN

'Ask Fawcett'—The Ancient Mariners and the Diplomat—Christmas Exceedings—Fawcett as Host—A Bore foiled—The British Association.

But if no respecter of persons, Fawcett unfailingly took every opportunity to play the good Samaritan. Were a friend in trouble, this great rough comforter was the first at hand to help. If ill, he had probably from the beginning been sitting daily at the patient's bedside, bringing good cheer, or aiding in the thousand and one ways which his understanding of suffering, through his own great suffering, had taught him. Nothing gave him greater joy than to help in this way.

He was sent for on one occasion by an old gentleman on his deathbed.

'Ask Fawcett.'

The invalid had shared some of his guest's tastes, and before the interview ended the old man, instead of dedicating his last hours to spiritual things, became so cheered and animated by his blind friend that he called from his bed for his fishing-tackle and a bottle of his best port. This sudden convalescence so scandalised the family that the vitalising guest was not urged to call again. He was sure to give the heartiest, least morbid cheer, and revelled in his great privilege of service wherever it was needed, wherever he could enter. Moreover, his helpfulness was not spasmodic, it was continuous and unforgetting, and he was counted on as the most faithful and, in a homespun way, the most delicate of friends. It necessarily follows that he became a connecting link to a large circle of Cambridge friends. To the inquiry where any Cambridge man was, and how the fates were treating him, it was the usual thing to say, 'Ask Fawcett.' Whether the man had drifted away or had been wrecked financially, socially, or by bad health, the blind man always knew all about it, and had usually tried to set things right. He believed firmly in the need of 'keeping his friendships in constant repair.' He did not age prematurely and had the happy talent throughout life of seeing things from a youthful point of view. It was one of his principles to make friendships with younger men. Some of the most brilliant juniors found in him a warm and loyal comrade.

The Ancient Mariners and the Diplomat.

He joined a famous boat crew known as the Ancient Mariners, an entirely safe body of athletes not liable to over-exert itself. Fawcett's rowing was as vigorous as it was erratic. He could not keep time with the others, so they wisely made him stroke.

The Ancient Mariners shockingly beguiled a trusting diplomat sent by Napoleon III. to study Cambridge sport. The young envoy had just arrived at Cambridge and was taking in with close scientific observation all its characteristics. He paused while passing through the Backs as the Ancient Mariners stroked by Fawcett, skying horribly as was his wont, hove into sight. Full of interest, the Frenchman studied their movements, and was surprised when the learned body of professors passed at their aged and intellectual appearance. He spoke to two undergraduates standing by. '*Pardon, messieurs*, is that the famous Cambridge crew?' 'Yes,' solemnly responded one shameless youth. 'But, monsieur, they are very old.' 'Oh yes,' came the answer, 'the strain in training makes them so.' Pondering on this shocking fact, the Frenchman industriously made notes which were later digested by his compatriots. Unfortunately history has not given us his report to the Emperor on the Cambridge crew.

Trinity Hall.

Christmas Festivities.

Trinity Hall was founded in 1350 by the far-sighted Bishop Bateman. He had been greatly alarmed by the terrible black death, and wished to provide against a scarcity of lawyers. A more genial benefactor sought to leave a merrier bequest, and provided for an annual Christmas festivity, properly ushered in by chapel service and followed by a Latin oration—a eulogy on Civil Law. These Yule-Tide 'exceedings,' as they were gaily termed by the fellows, had a picturesque historic reputation, and are well described by Leslie Stephen, who enjoyed them to the full. He writes: 'It was almost a religious ceremony. If we could not rival the luxury of a civic banquet, there was an impressive solemnity about the series of festivities which lasted some ten days at Christmas time. The college butler swelled with patriotic pride as he arranged the pyramid of plate—the quaint little enamelled cup bequeathed by our founder, which had, I think, a shadowy reputation for detecting poison; the statelier goblet given by Archbishop Parker, which made its rounds with due ceremony that we might drink "in piam memoriam fundatoris"; and the huge silver punchbowl, which represented Lord Chesterfield's view of the kind of conviviality likely to be appreciated by the Fellows of his own period. The Master ... beamed hospitality from every feature as he presided at the table, prolonging the after-dinner sitting till the port and madeira had made the orthodox number of rounds.'

Fawcett loved these festivities, and rejoiced greatly when he could succeed in bringing his old friends back to Cambridge, where 'midst the clatter of forty pair of knives and forks and the talk of forty guests his ringing volleys of laughter would assert their supremacy.'

A friend adds: 'We used to argue whether Fawcett or one of his friends, whose lungs could emit a crow of superlative vigour, was capable of the most effective laughter; but if the single explosion of his rival was most startling no one could deny that Fawcett was superior in point of continuous and infectious hilarity.'

These Christmas functions would be accompanied by long expeditions, walking, riding, or when weather permitted, skating. Fawcett would never lose a chance of this last. A Cambridge companion has told that 'as soon as it was even frosty, Fawcett wanted to go skating. Even if no one else risked it he was glad to open the season. Once early in the winter he insisted on skating on the river Cam at Cambridge. We took a boy with us. It was very rough. We skated below the lock, where there is a long space of river with a strong current. It wasn't at all safe, and I was relieved when I was able to persuade Fawcett to come ashore. Scarcely had I succeeded when two undergraduates appeared on the river. "I don't see why I can't skate if they can!" said Fawcett. "They will be in the river in a minute," I replied, and so one of them was, and the boy whom we had taken with us and I were forced to become life-savers.'

He always remembered to carry pennies in his pocket for the man to put on his skates, or oranges for the children.

Fawcett as Host.

In 1859 Fawcett, who had recently opened a correspondence with Mill, hospitably asked him to the college Christmasing, but the great economist did not come. At different times Fawcett had many guests, notably Cobden, who came to see Fawcett in the summer of 1864 and charmed the Dons by his delightful urbanity. The great agitator was himself glad to make the discovery that Dons abate their political prejudice to be hospitable. Professor Huxley was also gladly welcomed by Fawcett, besides other scientists, politicians, economists, and lawyers, famous in their time, and who if not immortals now at all events did their share to create that great epoch of betterment in the English world, the Victorian era.

Fawcett had now become a well-known figure, and suffered the usual consequences. His strategy in self-preservation is described by one friend thus:

A Bore foiled.

'I was walking with him one day when he was stopped by the long conversation of a very uninteresting Professor. A few days later, when we were again walking, I told Fawcett of the approach of the same old bore. "How far off is he?" asked Fawcett. "About three hundred feet ... now about a hundred and fifty." Fawcett's pace kept quickening and quickening so that I could hardly keep up; when about twenty yards off his legs shot out like the huge pistons of an engine. I had to run to keep up with him. Like a flash of lightning we passed the Professor, Fawcett shouting as he sped furiously by, "How do you do, Professor? Very fine day. Good-bye"; and when the Professor in a few seconds was left a marvelling dot on the horizon, Fawcett turned to me and said, "He's even slower than he looks!"'

Fawcett revelled in Cambridge society, and constantly compared it with London, to its great disadvantage. He felt that no continuity was possible in the talk of London drawing-rooms, and that an enormous amount of time was lost in unnecessary pioneering before one could discover a ground of common interest. At last when you were established comfortably on this ground, you were briskly whirled away to repeat the tragedy in some other circle. He had no patience with the early break-up of London dinner-parties, owing to the custom of moving on to other functions, and he staunchly refused to go to 'At Homes.'

Cambridge Society.

In Cambridge life was so much simpler, men knew each other, so that no time was lost by preliminaries, and one could still have 'talk such as Johnson enjoyed at the Turk's Head.' One had only to walk across a court to meet old friends, to strike at once into the vital things one cared about. Here serious subjects were considered seriously, and by men who were young enough to feel what they had to say and hope that their opinions would jog the old world a little from its hackneyed course.

Stephen tells us how at Christmas time he would rejoice with Fawcett in an early and conversational breakfast; then discuss the newspaper until luncheon; the long afternoon tramp and talk would end just in time to prepare for dinner, and after dinner more smoking and argument until the wee hours of the next day. What a triumphant test of friendship and fluency!

Much of the ability of Fawcett to entertain — and be entertained — from morning until past midnight was the result of his talent for accepting the small and trivial things of life as legitimate pabulum for talk. He would begin a morning's conversation with, 'What did you have for breakfast to-day?'

Anecdotage.

He had a surprising avidity for anecdotes, and loved to hear certain lengthy ones repeated numberless times. He would listen, his attention glued to these worn tales, and would beg with an infantile eagerness to have some hoary story retold which he had heard over and over for a quarter of a century. His friend, the late Master of Jesus College, had a rare genius for mimicry of voice and gesture. Fawcett revelled in his performances; he would be on the *qui vive* with the delight of anticipation, and 'as the well-known anecdote proceeded every muscle of his body would quiver with enjoyment and he would end with laughter-choked petitions for more.'

Though Fawcett possessed a remarkably strong and rugged mind, his training reflected the limitations of the Cambridge curriculum of his day, in which the development of brain fibre by mental gymnastics and keen competition was the chief object.

The undeniable charm which accompanies the type of mind which is attracted by mystery or the more subtle forms of the æsthetic was denied to Fawcett. Though his biographers may feel that he would have been more interesting if he had possessed these qualities, the frank acceptance of his limitations and the record of his achievement make a story of such heroism that it requires nothing more than what legitimately belongs to it.

The short-sighted put him down as a Philistine, an epithet well described as that name which a prig bestows on the rest of the species; but between Fawcett and a prig there was a natural lack of harmony. He appreciated good work wherever he found it. The novels of George Eliot, the Brontës, or Jane Austen were a great delight to him. *Esmond* and *Vanity Fair* were read to him several times over, and he would ask for certain sonorous passages from Milton or Burke.

The British Association Meeting.

In 1860 he visited Oxford, where the British Association was holding its meeting. He read a paper in which he had the hardihood to attack the caustic Whewell, assailing his preface to the works of Richard Jones. A large meeting gathered to witness the encounter. 'Fawcett had learned by heart a sentence from Whewell's preface. Whewell replied and repudiated the phrases quoted. Fawcett slowly and accurately repeated the words, which Whewell again disavowed. Then Fawcett called to his secretary to produce the volume in which the unlucky sentence had been marked. The Chairman read it out, when Fawcett's quotation appeared to be perfectly correct. He thus gained an apparently conclusive triumph.' 'There were not a half-dozen people in the room,' Fawcett observed afterwards, 'who would have understood if I had got the best of the argument as to the inductive method; but they all heard the passage repeated distinctly three times.' Though the younger man had unquestionably routed this senior, Whewell took his defeat magnanimously, and was from that time on excellent terms with his conqueror.

CHAPTER X
THE YOUNG ECONOMIST

Championing Darwin—Darwin at Downe—Salisbury Gossip—Meeting Mill—Fawcett for Lincoln and the Union—John Bright's Dog—Chair of Political Economy.

Championing Darwin.

In consequence of that Oxford meeting Fawcett entered another arena. Bishop Wilberforce, representing the attitude of many not narrow-minded men, took that occasion to attack Darwin's recently published *Origin of Species*. Fawcett, indignant at the theological onslaught on the new theories, published an article in *Macmillan's Magazine* in which he valiantly took up the gauntlet for Darwin.

Now, when evolution has become so much a part of our accepted and automatic thought, when we realise that science can in no way disprove religion, but if anything recommends it on a scientific basis, making the wonder of creation more real, it seems quaint to remember and difficult to appreciate that in Fawcett's day the great evolutionist was hated as an iconoclast whose teachings would undermine religion, that Darwin was actually anathema to the orthodox and the pious minded.

Fawcett writes with his usual clearness, stating the true and logical position of Darwin's theory; distinguishing carefully between a fruitful hypothesis and a scientific demonstration; exhibiting the general nature of the argument and the geological difficulty with great clearness, and taking some pains to prove that religion is in no danger from Darwinism. In any case, he says, 'life must have been originally introduced by an act of creative will.' He restated these arguments at the next year's meeting of the British Association in Manchester. Although this controversy for his part went little further, it led to some correspondence with Darwin, from whose letters it is of interest to quote:

A Letter from Darwin.

My dear Mr. Fawcett,—I wondered who had so kindly sent me the newspapers, which I was very glad to see; and now I have to thank you sincerely for allowing me to see your MS. It seems to me very good and sound; though I am certainly not an impartial judge. You will have done good service in calling the attention of scientific men to means and laws of philosophising. As far as I could judge by the papers your opponents were unworthy of you. How miserably A. talked of my reputation, as if that had anything to do with it.... How profoundly ignorant B. [who had said that Darwin should have published facts alone] must be of the very soul of observation! About thirty years ago there was much talk that geologists ought only to observe and not theorise; and I well remember some one saying that at this rate a man might as well go into a gravel-pit and count the pebbles and describe the colours. How odd it is that any one should not see that all observation must be for or against some view if it is to be of any service!

I have returned only lately from a two months' visit to Torquay, which did my health at the time good; but I am one of those miserable creatures who are never comfortable for twenty-four hours; and it is clear to me that I ought to be exterminated. I have been rather idle of late, or, speaking more strictly, working at some miscellaneous papers, which, however, have some direct bearing on the subject of species; yet I feel guilty at having neglected my larger book. But, to me, observing is much better sport than writing. I fear that I shall have wearied you with this long note.

Pray believe that I feel sincerely grateful that you have taken up the cudgels in defence of the line of argument in the *Origin*; you will have benefited the subject.

Many are so fearful of speaking out. A German naturalist came here the other day, and he tells me that there are many in Germany on our side; but that all seem fearful of speaking out, and waiting for some one to speak, and then many will follow. The Naturalists seem as timid as young ladies should be, about their scientific reputation. There is much discussion on the subject on the Continent, even in quiet Holland, and I had a pamphlet from Moscow the other day by a man who sticks up famously for the imperfection of the 'Geological Record' but complains that I have sadly *understated* the variability of the old fossilised animals! But I *must* not run on. With sincere thanks and respect, pray believe me, yours very sincerely,

Charles Darwin.

Going to Darwin at Downe.

Fawcett was a great admirer of Darwin, and the famous scientist had a whole-hearted admiration for him, and thought most highly of his work on political economy. While Fawcett was staying with Lord Avebury they started on the tree-shaded lane that leads uphill to Downe, where Darwin lived, but Fawcett sped much too fast for his host, who had taken his arm. The blind man said, 'I don't need you to lead me; if you just keep close enough to me to prevent my going into the hedges, I am all right!' 'But I don't do it to guide you,' replied Lord

Avebury, 'I do it to help myself, you walk so quickly.' Fawcett was hugely amused, and the blind man continuing thus to lead the sighted, they arrived at Darwin's, where they had a very merry time.

At Salisbury.

It was a great relaxation and joy for Fawcett when he was able to spend a few days with his beloved family at Salisbury. He often took his work with him, and was forced at times to deny himself to visitors. One morning when he was at work an old lady called who had been his sister's schoolmistress. When, at luncheon, he heard that she had been there, and had asked for him, but that they had refused to interrupt him, he exclaimed, 'Oh, why didn't you call me for a friend?' Although he knew the old lady but slightly, and she had no claims on him, he was not happy until he had called on her that same afternoon and told her how sorry he was not to have seen her.

The Joy of Gossip.

It is refreshing to find that he was devoted to gossip, and in the home circle at Salisbury he would often ask Mrs. Fawcett pleadingly, 'Mother, can't you go out to hook a little news for me?' and the mother would sally forth in search of the latest village excitement. She had a talent, perhaps inherited by the son, of, to state it conservatively, making the very best of any anecdote; and when she returned to the picturesque stone cottage in the close, where she found her long son toasting himself before the fire in pleasant anticipation of a good dish of fresh gossip, great was their mutual satisfaction. Urged by him 'to tell it all without interruptions,' she would relate what she had absorbed with her neighbour's tea. She knew well how to give the flowery rendering that delighted her son. As the story increased in picturesqueness and interest, Fawcett, who had been bending forward, his lips slightly parted in anticipation of coming smiles, would rock back and forth with sheer glee. As the narrator skilfully made each point he would shout joyously, 'Bravo, mother! Bravo! go it, mother!' He would never let any one else retail the village talk. She gave it so much more point.

He could also 'hook news' for himself, and had a favourite tale culled from a Salisbury gossip. An old dairyman who was a great friend of his announced one day that they had 'a new, beautiful clergyman at Harnham.' 'What kind?' asked Fawcett. 'Oh, fine—he goes so terrible high and so terrible low!'

Though he retained his childlike curiosity, it is notable that he was absolutely free from ill-nature, and one of his intimates states that he never heard Fawcett say an ill-natured thing or intentionally spread a possibly mischievous rumour. Though he had a splendid contempt for certain weaknesses, he was always discreet, and tried his best to promote kindly feeling. His love of talk was so infective that it stimulated a flow in those who without him would have been reticent or silent.

Meeting Mill.

In Cambridge he used to be teased about his total lack of any embarrassment or shyness, but he would answer these sallies with, 'If you could ever see me meeting Mill, you would see me awkward enough!' The meeting took place, but not in the presence of these Cambridge cronies; and what happened was never known, as Fawcett kept this sacred mystery to himself.

In the letter, already mentioned, written to Mill in 1859, he says that he is 'personally a stranger to you,' and then alludes to 'the very kind sympathy you have expressed to me,' and continues:

Correspondence with Mill.

> For the last three years your books have been the chief education of my mind; I consequently have entertained towards you such a sense of gratitude as I can only hope at all adequately to repay by doing what lies in my power to propagate the valuable truths contained in every page of your writing.

He certainly was a deeply attached pupil.

He writes later:

> Pray accept my most sincere thanks for your letter; I cannot tell you how much I value your words of kind encouragement. Often when I reflect on my affliction, I feel that it is rash on my part to attempt anything like a career of public usefulness; and again and again, I am sure, my heart would fail me if it was not stimulated by your thoughts and teachings. I can therefore assure you that your kind words will remove many an obstacle to my course.

This allusion to his blindness and to the depressing effect that it had in making him doubt at times the practicability of his having a 'career of public usefulness' is as unusual for him as it is touching.

Even his iron will could not exclude the quiet moments when his disaster weighed on him with the force of its full burden, and he could not at all times banish a wistful expression which his friends grew to recognise when his face was not animated by talk or the stimulus of debate. It is even reproduced in some of the photographs, which show on his features the calm acceptance of a great tragedy.

Mill had not long lost the wife who had so radiantly coloured an otherwise grey existence, and doubtless the cordial admiration and the open-hearted friendship of the younger economist was very pleasant to him.

The pupil and master became great friends. Fawcett appreciated the gentle charm of the singular delicacy of feeling which he found under Mill's austere and aloof nature. At the unveiling in 1878 of Mill's statue, Fawcett said that Mill possessed qualities supposed to be the peculiar privileges of women, a gentleness and tenderness such as no woman could exceed. He revered his teacher so profoundly that it was sometimes thought that he was less generous in listening to the side of their common opponents.

In later years Professor Sidgwick, who ventured to find some flaws in the crystal, met with scant sympathy from Fawcett. Walking with a friend in Cambridge, Fawcett's attention was called to the nearness of Professor Sidgwick, apparently deep in conversation. 'Oh yes,' said he, 'there goes Sidgwick, carping on Mill.'

American Civil War.

While Fawcett was busying himself with the theory of economics in the quiet courts of Cambridge, its practice had given rise to a great conflagration in the Western Continent. The American Civil War raised many problems outside the country where it raged. England was considering where her sympathies lay. The Palmerstonian instinct to support a small state revolting against the possibly arbitrary insistence of a greater power gave one impulse in favour of the South; the grudging desire to see a large country split up gave another in the same direction. These were the feelings of the aristocracy and the press.

Lancashire Work People and Freedom.

But the Radicals and the common people had quite other thoughts. To them the great country in the West was the home and hope of freedom, and that it should strive to wipe itself free of the stain of slavery won the full sympathy of the freedom-loving people in the mother country. The working people of Lancashire stood by and starved that they might help America to be free.

In 1863 Leslie Stephen crossed the Atlantic. His letters to his mother were at his request all forwarded to Fawcett, who helped his friend by getting him letters of introduction.

Stephen writes, 'The letter which Fawcett got me from Bright to Seward proved very useful. It brought Seward down completely. Bright's name is (as Fawcett may tell him) a complete tower of strength in these parts. They all talked of him with extraordinary admiration.' And again, 'I also hear that old fox, Fawcett, with his customary low cunning, speaks complimentarily of my letters and suggests my writing a book on America.'

Fawcett for Lincoln and the Union.

Fawcett from the first was a strong Federalist, and both in public and in private spoke for the North. At Cambridge he was one of a small minority, and his rooms were the scene of many a battle for Lincoln and the Union.

HENRY FAWCETT AT CAMBRIDGE, 1863

From a contemporary painting in Trinity Hall

The other figures from left to right are Fawcett's guide, Professor Geldart
and Leslie Stephen

We have already commented on the curious resemblance, both physical and
mental, between the American and the Englishman. If we turn to the Trinity Hall
picture of Fawcett, Leslie Stephen, and others, the blind man's lofty top hat made
in England suggests the similar hideous head-gear which was worn by the American President at his inauguration, and which was humbly held by his conquered
adversary when the oath of office was taken by the victor. Fawcett is like Lin-

coln in his great wiry, lank length of six feet three inches or against the American six feet four inches; in their athletic force and power, as youths, they both threw their adversaries in wrestling bouts; their rusticity, simplicity, and felicity in ready speech; their unfailing love of fun and affection for small boys, animals, and all weak things in need of help. In their slight characteristics and in their great traits they had much in common; their sympathy, honesty, phenomenal patience and courage. They started on their careers with similar equipments—their great hearts and tremendous energies. They both, through vast suffering, found the road to a deep happiness, and with all their love and power they served their countries.

Hooking John Bright's property.

Fawcett's friendship for Bright has been referred to. It may not be out of place to repeat a favourite story Fawcett used to tell against himself of a fishing exploit in Bright's company. They had had no luck, and Bright was walking ahead along the river bank when Fawcett called out exultantly, 'Oh, Bright, I've got a big one!' He pulled hard. Bright turned round and exclaimed, 'Yes, indeed, you have caught your hook in the long hair of my dog,' and went to the rescue of the mystified collie, who was trying to extricate himself from Fawcett's vigorous fishing-line.

Friendship with Macmillan.

Largely at the instigation of his friend and future publisher, Macmillan, Fawcett began to write his first book on political economy in 1861. Alexander Macmillan was a great friend of Fawcett and of his circle. He often came to Fawcett's rooms to ask him and to persuade him to contribute some articles to the early numbers of *Macmillan's Magazine*.

It is possible that these two were drawn to each other by their great differences—Macmillan to Fawcett's strong, dogged common sense, and Fawcett to that esoteric vein in his friend's mentality. The following incident brings out strongly this contrast. Macmillan was popular with the graduates, who often spent interesting evenings at his house. One day he in turn was their guest in the Common Room. He held the floor in an extremely metaphysical conversation. Fawcett, who cared little for such talk and always said that philosophy ran off him like water off a duck's back, showed scant interest in the proceedings. Macmillan became more and more introspective and transcendental, and finally exclaimed, 'I often wonder, Fawcett, what I am here for,' to which Fawcett cheerfully replied, 'O Macmillan, we all know what you are here for—to bring out another edition of Hamblin Smith's *Arithmetic*.'

Manual of Political Economy.

Fawcett's *Manual of Political Economy* appeared early in 1863, when he was in his thirtieth year. He regarded his book merely as an introduction to Mill's larger work, which he said 'will be remembered as one of the most enduring productions of the nineteenth century.' The manual was very well received, and opened the way for Fawcett to succeed the then Professor of Political Economy, Professor Pryne, who was in failing health. On the death of this gentleman the choice for a successor lay among four candidates. The great ability of one of these, then Mr. Leonard H. Courtney, now Lord Courtney, was already recognised. As, however, residents were preferred to strangers, the real contest was reduced to the two local candidates, Fawcett and Mayor. Fawcett's book was his chief asset in the struggle, and it, together with his discussion at the London Political Economy Club, of which he was a member, constituted the chief claims urged by his many influential friends throughout the country. They wrote the usual laudatory letters, but with perhaps more than the usual heartiness. Nevertheless, his blindness seemed a probable barrier to his ambition. Even one of his dearest friends refused to uphold his claims, feeling that a blind man could not properly fill the post, and there was much sincere doubt whether a man who could not see could keep order in his lecture-room. In addition to this, Fawcett's frank Radicalism counted against him; he had already, as we shall see in a later chapter, twice been a candidate for Parliament in the Liberal interest, the last time in Cambridge itself.

Candidate for the Chair of Political Economy. |

Such was the reputation for extreme opinions Fawcett and Stephen had given by their connection with Trinity Hall, that a certain country squire of ancient lineage and Conservative principles hesitated whether he dared send his son to the college where his ancestors had gained their learning. He decided to visit Cambridge, and there interviewed Stephen and Fawcett. He told them with unfeigned horror of the serious charges of Radicalism against the college that made him afraid to entrust his son to its keeping. The grave fellows compared notes solemnly before answering the father, then Fawcett reassured him, saying that the rumours which he had heard had been much exaggerated, and though at one time 'some of us had been rather infected with extreme opinions, now we have greatly moderated our views, and shall be content simply with the Disestablishment of the Church and the abolition of the Throne.' The immediate flight of the horrified squire can be imagined.

Elected.

Undismayed, however, Fawcett and his friends went to their electioneering with an astuteness and enthusiasm that vanquished all opposition, and on 28th November 1863 Fawcett was elected to the professorial chair. A jubilant letter was despatched by him to his mother the day after the election on 28th November 1863:

> MY DEAR MOTHER,—I hope you duly received the telegram. The victory yesterday was a wonderful triumph. I don't think an election has produced so much excitement in Cambridge for years. At last excitement was greatly increased by its being made quite a church and political question. All the Masters opposed me with two exceptions, but I was strongly supported by a great majority of the most distinguished resident Fellows. My victory was a great surprise to the University. I thought on the whole that I should win, but I expected a much smaller majority. Clarke however was very confident. He managed the election splendidly

for me, and curiously predicted that I should poll exactly ninety votes, and made a bet with Stephen that I should beat Mayor by ten to twelve. We are going to publish a list of the votes, which I shall send to you. My great strength after all was in Trinity. This says much for the independence of the College, as the Master was one of my strongest opponents....

All my friends in town regard it as a great political triumph. The Forsters [who had supported him in the election at Cambridge] were in a wonderful state of delight, and I have been overwhelmed with congratulations. I must now conclude, as I have many more letters to write. Give my kindest love to Maria, and believe me to be, dear Mother, ever yours affectionately,

HENRY FAWCETT.

THE PROFESSOR OF POLITICAL ECONOMY

'A man may see how this world goes with no eyes.'

Shakespeare.

'He that hath light within his own dim breast
May sit i' the centre, and enjoy bright day.'

Milton.

CHAPTER XI
A PROGRAMME OF HELPFULNESS

The Triumph over Blindness—The Professor's Audience—Free Trade
and Protection—The Luxury of Light—The Malady of Poverty.

The Triumph over Blindness.

His election to a professorial chair meant much to Fawcett and helped greatly to carry him successfully forward in the career which he had mapped out for himself. It proved two points of much significance in his life as a blind man: first, that his colleagues and the elder men in authority at Cambridge thought that he had the intellectual training and qualifications to develop the honourable post to which he was elected; and secondly, that they did not feel that his blindness would hinder his making the most of his knowledge or prevent his students reaping good results from his lectures. Perhaps no less important was the added buoyancy and confidence given to Fawcett by a knowledge of his ability to control and lead men, even if they were only his pupils at Cambridge. This was a step, even if a very small one, on his path towards his election to Parliament. From that point of vantage he felt that he could ultimately lead the hosts of the ignorant and oppressed and force great issues for the national welfare.

The material advantages following his victory were also important: his fellowship yielded from £250 to £300 a year, which, with his professorship worth £300 a year, was sufficient for his needs. He rejoiced that his professorship compelled him to be at Cambridge for eighteen weeks each year, and for the rest of his life he continued to give his annual course of lectures.

The attitude taken towards the duties of a professor at Cambridge at that time seems to us now almost comic and Gilbertian. It was not expected that the professor should have a voluntary attendance of enthusiastic pupils at his lectures. When it was considered advisable for him to have a larger audience, the lecture-rooms were filled by forcing the 'poll' men, that is the undergraduates taking the Ordinary Degree, to attend a certain number of lectures; and whilst this arrangement remained in force Fawcett had a large share of these coerced auditors. In 1876 the regulation was done away with, and his lectures were nearly deserted, though in his later years he had again a respectable audience.

The Professor's Audience.

A friend who saw Fawcett lecturing at Cambridge after the repeal of compulsory attendance says that the impression made upon him was grotesque. On entering the lecture-room, which was practically deserted, one saw the huge blind man holding forth with his ringing voice to space. Fawcett, in answer to condolences on this weird phenomenon, replied, with a merry laugh, that it was quite all right and he was used to it.

Fawcett was practically the only professor who objected to the withdrawal of compulsion; he said that he had been convinced by experience that his hearers profited more than he had anticipated. Examinations showed that they had really acquired useful knowledge. He did not share the objections of his colleagues, who felt that they had to lecture above the capacities of their enforced audiences. He should not, he said, alter in any case the character of his own lectures. There is something sublime and adamantine in this attitude; with his two feet planted firmly, the blind man proposed not for a moment to lessen the height of his intellectual stature, but by sheer force and determination, derrick-like, to hoist even the lowest members of his audience up to his own level. The impracticability of this point of view is obvious, but it is intensely Fawcettian. He felt that the great truths embodied in political economy were so simple and vital that he could graft them painlessly and with good results on the most unfertile mind.

The Science of Helpfulness.

He did not confine himself to elucidating the essential elements of his science only, nor was he content to reiterate what he had said to former audiences. He loved political economy as a living and helpful science. His lectures were always fresh, earnest, and illustrated by the bearing of the subject on history or current political events. He did not care to teach subtleties, but to drill his pupils in a science which he firmly believed would help them to deal intelligently and efficiently with the great problems of inequality, poverty, ignorance, and misery which were calling in vain to high Heaven to be solved.

Fawcett's critics among the younger men often felt that he was too conservative. He idealised Mill, and his friends maintained that he had read no book except Mill's *Political Economy*; it was true that he had read no book so exhaustively. He urged his hearers at one of his lectures to study some good book until they were prepared to give the substance and fully to analyse the argument of every chapter, and then having acted conscientiously on his advice himself, naïvely suggested Mill's *Political Economy* as excellent for this purpose.

Homely Political Economy.

He proved the teachings of Ricardo and Mill by what he had learned from the conditions of the country folk about Salisbury and Cambridge. He was wont to base his arguments on some homely, definite fact as illustration for his plain, home-made reasoning; for instance, he objected to a certain increased tax because it meant that every old woman in England would have a lump of sugar the less in her tea. That was the concrete thing on which he based his policy; and surely it is not one to be overlooked by a true statesman. He supplemented his knowledge by studying inexhaustibly the political, financial and economic movements of his time, and delighted in spending a quiet Sunday reading through all the newspapers he could collect. His appetite for them was insatiable, and he felt that he had been defrauded if his friends, when reading the Parliamentary debates, skipped any of even 'the blow off,' as they called the peroration.

He enriched his mind less by a pre-occupation with the abstract theory of Political Economy than by keeping constantly in touch with the affairs which were in actual course of transaction.

Free Trade and Protection.

He was keenly interested in all those questions where political economy borders on finance. His book, *Free Trade and Protection*, published fifteen years after his first, assailed the tariff fetish dear to his generation. Terse and masterly, his publication became popular, and was regarded by many of the critics of his day as conclusive. In it he limited the problem to what he deemed its practical viewpoint. To him this was purely a commercial one, a question of profit and loss. Was protection profitable or not? He found that, sporadic evidence at times to the contrary, protection was not a paying business, and that it would only be maintained in the long run by a loss to the community, and therefore he considered it an obstruction in the way of progress, capital, and the general weal.

The Luxury of Light.

He was impressed by the fact that the evil of the day was the hopeless poverty of the mass of the people. He felt that the only way to help them was to understand the principles that govern 'the conditions and consequences of money making and money spending,' and so discover how best to make it possible for them to earn more money, that is, to have more power in exchange. He felt that men should be less content with their lot, and that schools and savings banks to replace the public-house would be great factors for regeneration. He used to tell the following anecdote, which touched his friend Mill deeply. Fawcett knew a Wiltshire man who was in the habit of going to bed at dusk. The man explained that this was his custom because he could not afford a candle, and added that, even if he could, he could not read, so why should he have the expense or luxury of light? How was it possible to change this labourer's horizon, to lift him beyond the degrading pressure of sordid poverty, and to fill him with ambition, when he had to support his wife and himself on nine shillings a week? 'Let us endeavour,' Fawcett says, 'to understand the true causes of poverty. That is the vital problem.'

Malady of Poverty.

As a Professor of Political Economy he tries, like a careful doctor, painstakingly to study and understand the symptoms of the malady of poverty and misery, refusing to accept any superficial diagnosis. He wants to discover the cause of the disturbance which, like a malignant tumour, vitiates the whole social system. While coping with these problems he kept his mind cool, critical, and impersonal, refusing all quack remedies, and seized every detail that helped him to his goal. In all simplicity he once asked Leslie Stephen why Carlyle called political economy the 'dismal Science'—not a difficult question for the average man! But Fawcett loved budgets and balance-sheets; they brought to his mind vivid, concrete pictures that could never be dull, and he studied them industriously; industriously enough to realise thoroughly the fallibility of figures and the old truth so often quoted (can the reader bear it again?) that there are three kinds of lies, 'Lies, Damned Lies, and Statistics.' Though his respect for his forerunners was great, his beliefs were fearlessly his own.

His warm personal relations with country labourers, many of whom he called his intimate friends, never lessened. Once, after a day's fishing at Salisbury with Wright, he had some beer with a farmer, who told him that the labourers' wages were to be lowered after the harvest. Fawcett, after vainly protesting, refused more beer and walked home. On his way he met one of his labouring friends, who accounted for his best clothes by saying that he was going to a harvest-home celebration at the church. Fawcett fell into a long reverie, and at last asked Wright how he would like to give thanks for a bountiful harvest when his wages were to be docked of a shilling a week.

Co-operation.

Such facts touched him deeply and set him pondering and writing on how best they could be changed. Co-operation seemed to him to be the cure for these ills; he felt that it would bind together the interests of the capitalists and the working men, and would ultimately do away with the friction between them. An article he published on this subject attracted the notice of George Eliot, and his proposals were put into practice at a colliery near Leeds.

CHAPTER XII

THE SCHOOLS OF THE POOR

Need of Non-Sectarian Education — Charity and Pauperism — Friendship with Working Men — The Voice that linked.

Need of Non-Sectarian Education.

But co-operation without intelligence and education in all classes was impossible. Fawcett felt keenly the need of non-sectarian national education, especially for the rural population. Schools would enlighten the workman so that he could learn how to make his work more profitable to himself and others, and how to make the best of his free hours, and so work out his independence.

To the argument that compulsory school attendance, when the schooling was not gratuitous, would impose additional burdens upon the poor, he replied that the wages of labourers were determined not by open competition, but by what was absolutely necessary to keep soul and body together. The payment for schools would therefore not come out of their pockets, but be made up in their wages. The employer would be reimbursed either by a reduction of his rent or, it might be confidently hoped, by the increased efficiency of labour. A man considers himself repaid for keeping his horses in good condition, whilst he leaves his labourers in a state of semi-starvation. Fawcett held that whatever would give and stimulate the best in men was good, but he abhorred all that tended to restrict the independence and freedom of action of the poor.

Charity and Pauperism.

This latter principle made him a strong opponent of any form of State regulation of the lives and labour of the adult poor. It seemed to him that charity unsafeguarded which inevitably increases pauperism. He realised that tyranny always tries to justify itself; his interest in America made him familiar with the doctrine that slavery is best for the slave. 'Interference may be tyranny in disguise even when it is really based on the best motives.' He wrote sternly against State socialism and the nationalisation of the land. These plans, he said, regarded the State as a kind of supernatural milch cow, a body capable of making something out of nothing, of directly commanding supplies of manna from the heavens and water from the rocks; whereas, in point of fact, these were simply schemes for taking money from the prudent and handing it over to the idle.

In his search for practical solutions to these questions he put himself in close touch with the individual workman and his conditions, as well as with Trade Union officials. When at Bradford, during a strike against the introduction of new labour-saving machinery, the blind man went fearlessly among the excited workmen and cautioned the men against driving away their trade by their methods. He strongly denounced violence, and arguing calmly to these under-fed, discontented men, he compelled their interest; they listened, and were largely convinced by his logic and good-will. Many working men regarded him as their hero and champion.

Recently a London locksmith told the writer that he was a member of the Henry Fawcett Club for Workmen, and that one of their proudest memories was that Fawcett had at one time addressed the club and taught it great principles of life and work.

Friendships with Working Men.

The working men and women appreciated what his friendship meant, and felt that there was no one who could better speak for them.

Odger.

George Odger, a shoemaker, the first workman to stand for Parliament, was a great friend of Fawcett's. He used to tell this tale of his candidature. It was before the ballot, and it was the custom to publish the state of the poll from time to time throughout the day. There were two Conservatives and two Liberals standing for two seats, and Odger standing as an independent working-class candidate. As the day went on it became clear that one of the Liberals would be returned, but that if the second Liberal and Odger held on a Conservative would win the second seat. Fawcett and some other Liberal politicians went more than once to the Liberal Whip's headquarters, and implored him as the chief of the Liberal party organisation to allow the second Liberal candidate to withdraw from the contest, and thus both save a seat for the Liberal party and allow a workman to get in. Out of dislike to a working-class candidate, the party leader refused. The result was that both Odger and the second Liberal were defeated and a Conservative got in; and also a lasting bitterness on the part of Odger and his sympathisers towards the wire-pullers of the Liberal party, and apparently an enduring affection for Fawcett.

Frank Fairness.

At one of his political meetings, years after, Odger appeared to make a speech in defence of his friend, about whom he said, that if he or any other working-class leader went to see the professor in the House of Commons or elsewhere to ask him for his support for some Bill or proposal in which they were interested, Fawcett would not keep them standing in the lobby as some members would, but would receive them in the most friendly and unassuming manner. If he didn't agree with their proposal he would tell them so in the clearest and most direct terms, so that they always knew where they stood with him; if he agreed with them and thought them right he would back them through thick and thin, and if he thought their views unsound he would with equal candour tell them so and oppose them.

Odger had shown the same liking for plain speaking when he was present at the extraordinary meeting held during Mill's election for Westminster. In an essay in which he compared the working classes in different countries, Mill had said that in England the working classes were generally liars. At this meeting Mill was publicly asked if he had made the statement. Mill replied, 'I did.' His courage was received with a great burst of applause, and Odger, who spoke next, said that the working classes wanted friends not flatterers, and were truly obliged to any one who could treat them so straightforwardly.

Friendship till Death.

When, years later, Odger lay dying in the slums of St. Giles, Fawcett went to his bedside, giving what comfort he could, and an unfailing sympathy. When the old man died, Fawcett went to his funeral in Brompton Cemetery. His secretary, who accompanied him, gives this description, it was 'a long walk in a procession of many thousands, with trade bands playing funeral marches, alternating with the Marseillaise, and the banners of working-class organisations flying. We joined the procession in Knightsbridge and walked all the way to Brompton, and the throng at the cemetery was immense. Mr. Fawcett and I were dragged through the crowd to the grave, where the leader who had arranged the procession insisted on his making a short speech in eulogy of their dead comrade.'

A characteristic glimpse of Fawcett and his surroundings at this time is given to us by one of his sympathisers, who says:

'The first time I saw Mr. Fawcett was at a meeting summoned, as I understood, by himself, for the purpose of hearing an address from him on some subject connected with political economy and the interests of the working class. I was introduced to Mr. Fawcett after the lecture. Neither he nor anybody else had ever heard of my name at that time, but he was as frank and friendly as if we had met before and had known each other. He told me he was determined to try for a seat in the House of Commons, and he added cheerily, "I know I shall get a seat there some time."

'I did not meet him again for more than a year, it may have been two years, after. I happened to sit next to him at a small meeting of politicians and philanthropists. Mr. Mill was at the same meeting. We had the Reform question to interest us, the question between the Northern and Southern States of America, the question of legislation affecting the position of working men, the Irish question. Radicalism was then at once curiously robust and "viewy," a combination of qualities which politicians of a more recent birth find it perhaps a little difficult to understand. Mr. Mill belonged to some of our fraternities. Mr. Herbert Spencer was at one of them, at least. Mr. Huxley rather later came into one or two.

The Voice that linked.

'Some speaker got up who spoke well, and whom I did not know, and I asked Mr. Fawcett who it was. He told me promptly, and then to my surprise addressed me by name, and reminded me of the fact that we had talked together after his speech in St. Martin's Hall. His power of recognising men by the sound of their voices was something wonderful. Seventeen or eighteen years afterwards, I happened to sit two rows of benches behind him in the House of Commons. The House was nearly empty. Fawcett had spoken a few words on some subject of interest in India. When he sat down I uttered one quiet "Hear, hear." In a moment he turned towards me, and addressing me by my name, asked me whether I had seen a friend of his, the late Sir David Wedderburn, anywhere in the House that evening.'

The Call of the Outside.

However great his absorption in political affairs, Fawcett never forgot to satisfy his craving for fresh air and exercise. His sanity of outlook on serious things was largely due to his power of throwing them aside to enjoy a long tramp, a ride or a wintry skate. His nerve never failed him. One frosty day he walked across the frozen fens from Cambridge to Newmarket. The country is intersected with dikes and at any moment it was possible to plunge beyond one's depth into a half-frozen ditch. To Fawcett this was part of the fun, but his companion was far more anxious, and said that the Victoria Cross had been won by deeds requiring no greater courage and strength than this feat required of a blind man. Fawcett had learnt his lesson that for him life without courage was no life, and he habituated himself to hourly risks.

In company with a seeing confederate, he would have made a good scout. His knowledge of the country, of the mysteries of the woods and fields, intensified as he grew older. In the Wilderness, many an Indian path-finder would have lost the crackling of the branches under the swift hoof of a distant hurrying deer, or the soft call of the partridge to her young which Fawcett always heard. The distinctive smells and sounds of the seasons were clearly marked for him. The swish of the rollicking crisp leaves dancing before the wind along the roadways, and the thud of the falling apples on the hard ground in the orchard, made him laugh as it brought autumn to his senses. Winter, with its clear-cut noises, cracklings of ice and snow under foot, lost none of its sternness because he could not see its long white robes. He loved the smells of spring, and seemed to feel the pushing and striving in the dank earth and to divine the fragrance soon to burst forth. Like a giant lizard he revelled and basked in the heat of the summer sun, and rejoiced in the contrast of the cool shadow beneath the heavy-laden trees, the smell of the hot grass and of fully opened fragrant flowers, and the sedate 'brum' of the bourgeois bumble-bee.

Increasing Interests.

Though by his professorship attached for life to Cambridge, Fawcett's interests were deep in the world of politics, in which he had already made his début as the member of Parliament for Brighton. To simplify our story we will take up the history of his early political efforts in a new chapter.

The new M.P. was extremely popular; his friends were among the greatest men of the day—three of them at least, Darwin, Mill, Thackeray, gave new life to widely different callings.

CHAPTER XIII

THE NEW M.P. AND THE CLUB

Thackeray and the Reform Club—The popular M.P.—The Assassination of Lincoln—Marriage.

Thackeray as Champion.

As Fawcett was often in London, his friends were anxious for him to belong to a club. He was put up for membership at the Reform Club, but to the chagrin of his friends, the committee was loath to admit a blind man. It felt that he would be helpless and in the way. It delegated a member to tell Fawcett tactfully the feeling in the matter. He received the news with entire good humour and calmness, remarking quietly that 'every club has a perfect right to elect, or to refuse to elect, whomever it chooses on whatever ground it pleases.' But the attitude of Thackeray, who was a member of the club, was quite different; he felt the ruling was outrageous, and said so, exclaiming 'It is ridiculous—if Mr. Fawcett is only brought into the dining-room or the library every one of us there will forget that he is blind, and he will find his way about without any difficulty.' Vigorously taking up the cudgels, Thackeray routed all prejudice against his friend, and Fawcett was enthusiastically elected a member of the Reform Club. He received this news of success with the same genial calm with which he had before received that of failure.

It was a great disappointment to him that Thackeray, whom he had asked to the Christmas dinner at Trinity Hall in 1863, was unable to come owing to illness. Lady Ritchie remembers her father's desire to go to Cambridge for the famous festivity, and his regretful shake of the head as he said, 'No, I must give it up.' Lady Ritchie adds, 'We were so sorry for him, and also because he admired Mr. Fawcett very much.'

Overwhelmed with invitations, he had a tremendously good time wherever he went. If he was dining out, he would sometimes arrive at his host's a little before dinner, and ask to be shown to the dining-room and to have the places where each guest was to sit pointed out to him; he never forgot his lesson, so that during dinner he was able to speak quite naturally, turning as if he saw to any one at the table, addressing them by name. His conversation was delightful, and he had a marvellous faculty of putting people at their ease. On one occasion his hostess was absent when her guests arrived; a general formality and stiffness pervaded the circle until Fawcett arrived and at once broke up the ice and substituted a genial and comfortable glow of friendliness.

The popular M.P.

We have noted how he remembered people instantly by their voices, even if many years had elapsed since an only hearing. To him every woman seemed both charming and unforgettable. A friend tells how his wife, who had not seen Fawcett for many years, entered the drawing-room at a large reception. Although Fawcett was at the other end of the large room, he at once disentangled the lady's voice from the web of the general conversation, and threaded his way through the crowd to speak with her.

It is worth pausing a moment to think what an exquisite sense of hearing this story implies. What must the roar of a political mob have been to an ear of such delicacy?

At this time, all who saw Fawcett were not only drawn to him by his delightful and frank personality, but arrested by his strikingly interesting appearance. Like Saul, his fine head towered far above the people, his commanding height dominated any gathering. A great shock of blond hair at this time added picturesqueness to his strong face, and his vibrant voice roused all by its very earnestness; in intimate talk he spoke rapidly, riveting attention by his complete sincerity.

Though truly a mighty talker, Fawcett had the rare accompanying grace of absorbing himself in the conversation and interests of others. Furthermore, his blindness, by quickening all his remaining faculties, enabled him to hear without effort everything going on around him.

The Lure within.

The chatter in the brilliant drawing-rooms, the swish of silks, the trailing of velvets on silken carpets, the rustle of starch and frills on the parquet floor, the perfume used by the women, the smell of furs, candles, lamps and the warm air heavy with fragrant flowers, the murmur of distant fountains and music—everything touched the sensitive nervous organism. Transmitting quickly hundreds of impressions to his swift brain and wonderful imagination, they created for the blind man vividly the scenes in which he moved, and in which he delighted with greater keenness than the usual seeing person, and probably even more intensely than if he had seen them actually with his bodily eye.

Lincoln's Assassination.

He must have been in a listening mood one evening at a reception in London, when he suddenly heard a girlish voice, vibrant with tense emotion, say, 'Oh, it would have been better if every crowned head in Europe had been shot, than Lincoln!' The voice belonged to Miss Millicent Garrett, a girl of eighteen, who had just heard of Lincoln's assassination. Fawcett, too, was deeply moved by this news, and asked to meet Miss Garrett. He found himself at once with her on a common ground of sympathy, not only in the loss of the great emancipator, but in a deep admiration for the lofty principles of liberty for which Lincoln had given his life.

This meeting was the beginning of a rare understanding between two strangely harmonious and independent natures, and in the autumn of 1866 Fawcett became engaged to Miss Garrett, whom he married on April 23, 1867. Mrs. Fawcett was the daughter of Mr. Newson Garrett of Aldeburgh. The following notice of the event is taken from the *Suffolk Mercury* of the day:

'The commanding figure of the bridegroom, which towered above the surrounding gentlemen, bespoke him one of the tallest as well as one of the most distinguished of his countrymen.

'Amongst the most interesting of the wedding presents were a massive repeating chronometer, sent by the Fellows of Cambridge University, and a beautiful silver inkstand, the gift of one of Mr. Fawcett's constituents at Brighton.'

HENRY FAWCETT AND MRS. FAWCETT

Marriage.

The marriage of Fawcett did more to help him realise his ambitions and develop his intellectual abilities than any other event in his life. He used to say that he fell in love with his wife's mind, but from this we must not imagine that she lacked personal charm and a vivacious sense of humour. Their affection rested on a strong foundation of common principles and interests and of the love of freedom and justice.

A vivid impression of this unique and romantic couple is sketched for us in the accompanying story told by Lord Avebury.[2]

Sir John Lubbock, as he then was, was waiting at the Railway Station on his way to Wiltshire, when his attention was called to a reserved compartment decorated gaily with flowers. On asking the station-master to explain this unusual phenomenon, he was informed that the compartment was reserved for Professor Fawcett and his bride, who were about to start on their wedding trip.

A Trio and a Wedding Trip.

Just then Fawcett loomed in sight, his little girlish bride hanging on his arm. Sir John tried to vanish, but Fawcett's marvellous intuition had already detected his presence, and the blind man cried out in that voice which scorned concealment: 'Hello, Sir John, I want you to meet my wife. We are going on our wedding trip; you must come along!'

Willy nilly, Sir John was seized by the giant and hustled after the bride into the beflowered compartment. Much embarrassed, he protested as best he could, and tried to extricate himself, but Fawcett would not hear of it, and insisted on his accompanying them upon their wedding trip. Sir John made another heroic effort for flight, but just then the guard slammed the door, and he was forced to form a third for a part of the honeymoon.

This cordiality to his friends on all occasions was one of Fawcett's chief characteristics. He could not imagine any one whom he liked being in the way; and his wife's sense of fun always managed to make what might have been otherwise a difficult situation amusing and acceptable.

For the honeymoon Fawcett had taken a small cottage at Alderbury. The country had been familiar to him when he was there as a schoolboy. Each day he took his bride on some new and lovely drive, stopping on the way to show her the views which he loved and so well remembered.

Mrs. Fawcett.

Mrs. Fawcett had been before her marriage deeply interested in the questions of social interest which absorbed Fawcett. She had his entire sympathy both in her independent work as a political economist and in her championship of woman suffrage.

---

[2] The above was given to the writer by the late Lord Avebury at his home in London in 1911; it is taken directly from the notes made at the time.

After their marriage, they published together a collection of essays and lectures. Mrs. Fawcett's *Political Economy for Beginners* appeared shortly after, and quickly won its way to popularity. Fawcett was always eager in acknowledging his wife's help, and not only as his literary critic and editor. He valued her judgment in political matters more than his own, and would leave important questions unsettled until he had discussed them with her.

He gave a touching proof of his devotion and belief in her ability when a sudden accident threatened Mrs. Fawcett's life, and shook him out of his usual reserve. They had been riding together at Brighton, when Mrs. Fawcett was thrown violently from her horse. The fall knocked her senseless, and she did not regain consciousness for some time. The blind man could not be convinced that her stupor was not death, and that his friends, were not deceiving him. The grief and uncontrollable weeping of the big man were infinitely touching. He was so completely overcome that he had to give up an election meeting which he had expected to attend in the evening. On the following day, at a great assembly, he referred to his absence, and thanked the constituency for its previous support, saying that whatever difficulties he had met had been surmounted with the aid of others, and because he had 'a help-mate whose political judgment was much less frequently at fault than his own.' This was his attitude to his wife and her opinions throughout his life.

CHAPTER XIV

THE WOMAN AND THE VOTE

The Home in London—Sympathy with Woman Suffrage—The Blind
Gardener—Clubs—Hatred of Flunkeyism.

The Home in London.

His belief in Woman Suffrage probably began before he met his wife. It was
but a month after his marriage that he voted for Mill's motion in favour of ex-
tending the suffrage to women, the first time the question was introduced into the
House of Commons.

The hampered and restricted position of women industrially was a condition
that stirred Fawcett strongly. He felt that to bring the necessary pressure upon
legislation, women should have votes, and that much of the injustice from which
they suffered was due to their political powerlessness.

He loved a fight, and believed in competition to determine merit, but his spirit
revolted at the unjust restraint of the rights of mind and virtue by brute force. He
found that many paupers were women, and that their chance to support themselves was often negligible. So few wage-earning opportunities were open to them
that their employers were able to make what terms they pleased with these impov-
erished seekers for work. Poor women often gladly accepted wages which were
insufficient to hold soul and body together. Fawcett enthusiastically advocated
that women should be given a fair chance to do what work they could do well. He
spoke and worked to have women admitted to the examinations at Cambridge. He
did not attempt to dwell on the equality or inequality of man and woman, but con-
sistent with his lively sense of fairness, he felt that they should be given at least an
equal chance to develop whatever powers they had. The sad fate of the hundreds
of women whose lives were forced into useless inactivity depressed him: he did
what he could all his life to open many new fields to them.

Zeal for Fair Play.

His single-handed fight against a Bill restricting the work of adult women was
in the same direction. In this he took a very independent position. He considered
that restrictions on adult women were an infringement of their liberty, and that
it would probably have the effect of lessening their already narrow chances of
employment. His quickness to consider this second point was evidenced also in
his treatment of a question arising out of the bill for the compulsory registration

of teachers. A lady quite unknown to Fawcett wrote that it would tend to prevent many a young woman who was not regularly employed in teaching from adding to, or temporarily earning, her livelihood: he at once answered that that side of the question had not struck him, but that he would call upon her immediately to hear her statement of facts. Mrs. Fawcett, of course, augmented and shared her husband's natural enthusiasm for the enfranchisement of women. When she was asked to speak at Brighton on Woman's Suffrage some of his constituents objected, fearing that it would react unfavourably on Fawcett's political position, but he would not hear of preventing her carrying out her plan, and did then, as always, everything to help her in her cause.

Sympathy with Woman's Suffrage.

Since these pioneer efforts Mrs. Fawcett has been and is one of the strongest and most successful workers in a rational and dignified campaign for obtaining the suffrage for women. She and her daughter have effectively made great sacrifices for the cause which they have so much advanced by their eloquent enthusiasm and disinterested and legitimate efforts.

A most unusual honour has been accorded to Mrs. Fawcett. The portrait of Fawcett with his wife now hangs in the National Portrait Gallery, and is at this time the only portrait of a living woman, not of royal blood, in that historic collection.

The Blind Gardener.

Fawcett took his wife to live at 42 Bessborough Gardens. Later they went to live in The Lawn, Lambeth, where they stayed during the sittings of the House until his death. Despite the additional griminess due to the vicinity of Vauxhall Station, the Political Economist at once turned farmer on his estate of about three-quarters of an acre. He sent the asparagus which he raised within fifteen minutes' walk of the House of Commons, and which he insisted was a peculiarly good variety, to his father in Salisbury as proof of the excellent climate of London. Two small greenhouses furnished opportunity for raising flowers. These were an unfailing source of pleasure to the blind man, always keenly conscious of their beauty and gratified by their perfume. He knew them all by name and took pride in showing them to his guests. The old-fashioned house was made delightful by the artistic sense of Mrs. Fawcett. The happy couple were unmindful of the lack of social distinction inherent in their neighbourhood, and felt that the nearness to the Houses of Parliament, which were within pleasant walk along the river and over Westminster Bridge, as well as the horticultural opportunities, compensated their slender purse for any other shortcomings.

Radical Club.

A most fantastic incident occurred shortly after Fawcett's marriage which might have seriously affected his political career. His most sociable instincts had prompted him to found a club about the beginning of his first Parliament. It was called the Radical Club, and it consisted in equal numbers of politicians in and out of the House. Of course Mill joined. The club gathered influence. It met at weekly dinners, when the topics of the day were discussed. Soon afterwards Fawcett and his friends founded at Cambridge a new club, with the fearful name of Republican. It defined the name Republican as 'Hostility to the hereditary principle as exemplified in monarchical and aristocratic institutions, and to all social and political privileges dependent upon difference of sex.'

Republican Club.

The Republican Club was the means of promoting many delightful and charming dinners and evenings among a circle of brilliant and interesting friends. It was not a dark centre of conspiracy or revolution, and its members were not concocting a nineteenth-century version of the Gunpowder Plot. Unfortunately a weird and garbled account of the Club appeared in the papers and struck terror in the hearts of Fawcett's constituents. To them republicanism meant revolution and all the horrors depicted by Dickens in his *Tale of Two Cities*. One of Fawcett's best friends talked of making an amendment to the usual vote of confidence at the next Liberal meeting in Brighton. Though the proposed motion was given up, Fawcett profited by the opening to state clearly his principles; he said that he adhered to 'merit, not birth,' and denied any revolutionary predilections for his friends or himself, or any sentiment of disloyalty.

Hatred of Flunkeyism.

Fawcett was essentially a peace-loving citizen when peace and progress could go hand in hand. He had no plans for upsetting the monarchy, though he alone objected to the dowry voted by the House to the Princess Louise. He abominated flunkeyism as an aping of loyalty, and had no more regard for distinctions of rank than for differences of creed.

It is characteristic of him that while a democrat to democrats, he did not fall into the mistake of many broad-minded people, and forget that tact and congeniality are essential in bringing people together socially. He was very keenly alive to the differences in individuals, and took care that the gatherings at his house should be congenial and harmonious. When a proposed party was being plotted out he would say, 'Oh, don't ask the So-and-so's, they are such frumps.'

His very own Salt Cellar.

Mrs. Fawcett and he were delightful hosts; they liked having people at their house, and he greatly enjoyed his own as well as other folks' dinners. He was abnormally fond of salt, and to ensure an unfailing and adequate supply, carried a little sprinkling salt cellar with him, which he had carefully filled before dinner. He appreciated his food very much, and though not in any way a gourmand, paid full tribute to the high art of the cook.

THE NEW M.P.

' Darkness enwrapped him, yet with steadfast heart
He sought, unfaltering, the highest Ught.
His keen-eyed spirit failed not in the sight
Which sees, and seeing, loves the better part.'

PUNCH.

CHAPTER XV

BLIND SUPERSTITIONS

Speech before the British Association—Mill again—Bright and Lord
    Brougham—The Mythical Committee Room—Defeat at South-
    wark.

Blind Superstitions.

Fawcett never deviated from his school-boy longing for a political career. But despite the recognition which he had obtained as a speaker and thinker, even his best friends felt that his dream of a political future was worse than impracticable. They tried to dissuade him from his purpose, and make him content with a writer's life of study, thought and theory.

Opposition, the breath of life to this dauntless man, only added another stimulating obstacle to those he rejoiced to overcome—blindness, lack of money, and lack of distinguished origin. He had made up his mind to be a statesman before his accident; and he would in no wise falter. In the wonderful crucible of his genial kindliness, the opposition of his friends was distilled into a warm co-operation. He forced them to believe in his powers and future, and changed them into his enthusiastic political backers. His blindness, which appealed to the gentleness and pity of many, with him became a recognised force to help him to great feats of memory and prodigies of concentration. His very inability to read books and newspapers compelled him to cultivate his memory and tirelessly to think over the problems he wished to master. As a result of constant practice, he became able to memorise statistical information and use it in debate in a way which utterly baffled men of average ability. Even the most brilliant men of his day would have to use notes where Fawcett could trust to his memory alone.

A Telling Speech.

As we have said, a year after his blindness, with Brown to guide him, he went to Aberdeen, and spoke before the British Association. His paper there on the 'Social and Economical Influence of the New Gold' made a profound impression, and won him his first public recognition as an economist and statesman. He was much pleased with the result of his first effort in public, and the cordiality with which he was personally received.

But his sociability was not, as we know, confined to learned persons. During a journey he found himself in a small Scottish inn with a lonely dinner in prospect;

he was cheered to hear voices in the next room. He sent for the landlord and asked who was there. 'Some commercial gents,' was the reply. Fawcett asked the landlord to take his compliments to the 'commercial gents,' upon which he received an invitation to dine with them. He accepted with alacrity, and passed a most jovial evening in their company.

He next spoke at the Social Science Association at Bradford on the Protection of Labour from Immigration, and also on the theory and tendency of strikes. He made several loyal friends there, and his manifest ability led some of them to wish he might become a parliamentary candidate for a northern Borough.

The next year he acted as the member of a committee appointed by the Social Science Association, to investigate the problem of strikes. Lord Brougham and others of distinction were very friendly to him, though the veteran Reformer made some remarks about the American War which, Fawcett said, 'drove me half wild.'

Mill and a Political Opening.

In 1860 Fawcett was greatly encouraged by a meeting with Mill, who congratulated him on his choice of a political career. Mill considered that the blind man's loss of sight could only injure his prospects of political success if with sight zeal had also gone. The affliction could be turned into an asset which would arouse sympathy, and soften jealousies. Fawcett felt elated and stimulated by the older man's interest and belief in him, and lost no time in hunting for a political opening.

He interviewed Lord Stanley, but without results, for, as he reported to a friend, Lord Stanley 'thought me, I fancy, rather young.' And, after all, he was young—only twenty-seven—but he was determined. He watched for every chance of a bye-election, and knocked at the door of any borough where candidates seemed likely to be in requisition.

Bright and Lord Brougham.

When he asked Mr. Bright about some Scotch burgh, he was kindly but firmly advised to wait until his star had risen a little more above the public horizon. But Fawcett refused to lose time, and made his own opportunity. An article appeared in the *Morning Star* which stated that Southwark, then in need of a representative, had revolted against the control of its paid agents, and that a committee had been appointed to look for an independent candidate who would stand upon 'principles of purity.' The following morning Fawcett appeared before the committee. Bringing with him a letter from Lord Brougham, he introduced himself as 'of Norfolk Street, Strand, and a Fellow of Trinity Hall, Cambridge.' His declaration of principles was so satisfactory that the chairman of the committee consented to preside at a meeting.

First Political Meeting at Southwark.

Two good stories are told about this election. There is evidence to show that Fawcett himself set them in circulation. They curiously illustrate both his sense of fun and his shrewdness. One tells of his first meeting. This was held in an inn, and only one reporter came to it. Fawcett began chatting to him, asked him if he had anything special to do that evening, and then, as there was no audience, suggested to him to go home. He offered to send on a résumé of his speech. The reporter gratefully left, Fawcett then asked the landlord if there was any one in the 'parlour.' There were only a few commercial travellers, but Fawcett sent his compliments to them and asked them to come in. They joined him and all started a joyful evening together. In course of time, Fawcett asked one of the travellers if he would mind taking the chair, which he did. Fawcett then made a brief speech, and after drinks and a very merry time the party broke up, whereupon Fawcett wrote an account of the evening to his friend the reporter, giving the speech from the chair, which he of course made up, and his own oration.

As there was nothing particular doing, to Fawcett's surprise, the next day the London papers came out with a full account of the meeting at Southwark.

Fawcett went promptly to see the chairman of the previous evening, whom he found absorbed in the account of the great meeting. 'Why,' he exclaimed to Fawcett, 'I had no idea I made this speech last night. I have made speeches before, and I usually remember them! I only had a glass or two! I cannot see why I should have forgotten this one.' To which Fawcett replied quietly, 'You certainly have been well reported,' and left the bewildered orator to revel in his eloquence.

Lord Avebury said of this tale, which he had repeated to the writer: 'Tyndall was much shocked by this story, but I thought that the cleverness far outweighed the wickedness, and the humour of it appealed to me greatly.'

The Mythical Committee Room.

The other story tells of Fawcett's mythical committee room. It is to be remembered that he was quite unknown, and put himself up without support and with no possibility of winning.

He engaged a very small room and a very small boy to open its door. The candidate was rarely at headquarters, but his acolyte kept up appearances by informing any one who called that Mr. Fawcett was engaged with his committee.

The Contest.

He stood for a larger franchise; abolition of Church rates; removal of religious restrictions; economy; the volunteer movement; the equalisation of poor rates, and the reform of local government in London. He proved his principles of purity by refusing to pay a shilling to influence votes.

His success was immediate. The meetings that followed the first were crowded and overflowing. His interesting personality drew people from all parts of London to his meetings, till even the neighbouring streets were crowded.

But the other candidate entered the field. A campaign was started on behalf of a Mr. Scovell. This did not open with success. A meeting held for Scovell broke up in a pandemonium. Fawcett had the satisfaction a few days later of holding an orderly and overcrowded meeting in the very same hall.

The opposition now introduced a more formidable candidate in Mr. Layard (later Sir Austin Henry); the Government and the great employers were understood to favour him. This opposition seemed to decide the contest against Fawcett, and his friend Leslie Stephen says that he doubts if Fawcett ever seriously expected to go to the poll. Nevertheless he had his committee room duly placarded, though the candidate with his small attendant guide seems still to have been the committee. Fawcett spoke every night, and urged without success that a mass meeting of electors should choose between his qualifications and Layard's!

The Speaker's Eye.

Of course his opponents urged that Fawcett's obvious disqualification was his blindness, and that this was an insurmountable obstacle. The matter was hotly debated on both sides. All sorts of arguments were brought up at meetings and in the newspapers. How could a blind man decide questions about the laying out of streets? Fawcett showed how he could judge accurately of such things by putting pins in a map. How could he 'catch the Speaker's eye'? This objection amused Fawcett and his friends greatly. It is true that no member can raise his voice in the Commons unless able to perform that ceremony. But, as Fawcett gleefully explained, that mysterious ceremony consists in standing in one's place hat in hand, no difficult task for a blind man. It is for the roving eye of the Speaker to note the standing member and announce his name to the assembly. He thus gaily disposed of these objections, and cheerfully asked 'Mr. Layard to argue with him any point supposed to require eyesight,' when he would show his power of dealing with it.

Friends came forward to testify, at meetings and by letter, to his great abilities, and the editor of the *Morning Star*, which had treated his first speech so generously, delivered an eloquent oration in his favour.

Triumphant Defeat.

Fawcett fought that large borough for a month on less than £250. But the odds were too great, and he wisely decided not to go to the poll, where Layard obtained a majority of one thousand votes over Scovell.

Fawcett told a friend that this defeat would ensure him victory at the next contest. Notwithstanding his optimistic belief, he had still much to win through. He had shown his power of influencing a constituency, but he had still to overcome the scepticism in the minds of practical men as to the capabilities of a blind man, and to create for himself a support which could be counted on as a more positive factor than mere popular enthusiasm.

CHAPTER XVI

PURE POLITICS

Defeat at Cambridge and Brighton—Routing a Chimæra—Elected the
Member for Brighton—The House of Commons.

Fawcett's day was no more free from political chicanery and wire-pulling than
our own. Like all aspirants, he was sorely pressed to compromise with the un-
derworld of politics, but he kept himself clear of the political mire, and made no
promise which he could not justly fulfil.

The Flutter.

While waiting for his next chance his life was as usual busy and happy, labouring over papers for *Macmillan's Magazine*, editing his books, lecturing, and
generally leading the honest, frugal life of a man of letters. This quiet was diver-
sified by Fawcett's one and only 'flutter' in mining shares. His father had been for
some years working to retrieve the fortunes of a big mining undertaking in Corn-
wall. The son had been much interested, and accompanied his father on several
business journeys to the mine.

The elder Fawcett at last pulled his undertaking to a successful issue; this success gave a sudden fillip to mining shares. The son 'plunged,' and plunged with
success—so much so that he was seriously advised to give up politics, for the time
at least, and go on the Stock Exchange.

But he was not to be tempted by the lure of quick monetary success.

'I am convinced,' he said once, 'that the duties of a member of the House of
Commons are so multifarious, the questions brought before him so complicated
and difficult, that if he fully discharges his duty, he requires almost a lifetime of
study.' And again, 'If I take up this profession, I will not trifle with the interests
of my country. I will not trifle with the interests of my constituents by going into
the House of Commons inadequately prepared, because I gave up to the acquisition of wealth the time which I ought to have spent in the acquisition of political
knowledge.'

The sacrifice was unquestionable, and it emphasises his firm adherence to his
ideals, and his willingness to sacrifice great personal interests for the still uncertain career on which he had set his heart.

In 1863 a vacancy occurred in the representation of Cambridge. Fawcett's
friend, Macmillan, now came forward, begging Fawcett to issue an address, which

was circulated broadcast.

'Anybody's Candidate.'

'If I am anybody's candidate,' Fawcett said, 'I am Macmillan's candidate,' but he tried to be nobody's candidate.

His friends helped him vigorously, presiding or speaking at his meetings, or acting as his election agents.

Fawcett the elder came to support his son. Though the local papers assailed him, the most condemning assertions they could make were that Fawcett was an advanced Radical, who would abolish Church rates, though he professed to be a member of the Church of England; and worst of all, that he was capable of the crime of admitting Dissenters to Fellowships. How funny that latter accusation seems now, when the only question in obtaining a fellowship is, Has the man the brains to win it?

The Defeat at Cambridge.

Fawcett was defeated by eighty-one votes. The cost of the campaign had amounted to £600, but it had shown that Fawcett 'could go to the poll as well as make speeches.'

The election took place the same year that Fawcett was given the Chair of Political Economy, and made this latter honour all the greater, as it came despite his fearless Radical protestations.

The following January we find him coming forward as a Liberal candidate at a bye-election in Brighton. Three other Liberals presented themselves, and it was decided to have a meeting at which a committee, appointed by the electors, was to report on the merits of the candidates. The candidates should then address the meeting, and the decision was to be made by show of hands. But the committee managed ill, exceeding its instructions, and the meeting became a tumult. In the midst of the uproar Fawcett came forward and won probably the greatest oratorical triumph of his life. He began amidst great interruption, and after a few sentences the vast body of electors listened with breathless attention.

Routing a Chimæra.

Fawcett told them his story. 'You do not know me now,' he said, 'but you shall know me in the course of a few minutes.' He proceeded with the account of his accident, during which, says the reporter, 'a deep feeling of pity and sympathy seemed to pervade the meeting.' He told them how he had been blinded by two stray shots 'from a companion's gun'; how the lovely landscape had been instantly blotted out; and how he knew that every lovely scene would be henceforth 'shrouded in impenetrable gloom.' 'It was a blow to a man,' he said simply; but in ten minutes he had made up his mind to face the difficulty bravely. He would never ask for sympathy, but he demanded to be treated as an equal. He went on with the story of his previous attempts to enter Parliament, and ended with a profession of his political principles.

This account of the meeting is given by Stephen, who adds the comment: 'I do not think Fawcett ever again referred to his accident in public, except in speaking to fellow-sufferers. His blindness was apparently being made an insuperable obstacle; his best and most natural answer was to tell the plain story of his struggle, and he told it with a straightforward manliness which carried away his audience.'

The other candidates had spoken in a hesitating way about the attitude that England should hold towards the American Civil War. Fawcett began the political part of his speech by saying: 'Gentlemen, I am an uncompromising Northerner,' a statement that greatly pleased the meeting.

Sir Leslie helps.

Then the hard work of electioneering began. Fawcett set himself vigorously to the task, speaking effectively and often. His father and sister came to him to inspire and help as they could. His friend Leslie Stephen buckled on his friendly armour, and with all his love and great abilities did much to help in the brave campaign. He began by writing an article urging Fawcett's qualifications. It was refused in all the local papers, but this difficulty was gallantly surmounted. The editor of the *Morning Star*, who had supported Fawcett in his Southwark campaign, lent sufficient type; a room was taken, and the *Brighton Election Reporter* started a brief but brilliant career. Leslie Stephen became editor and moving spirit in chief. The publication was sold at a halfpenny a copy. Was it shrewdness or love for boys—for both were in Fawcett in full measure—that determined that the newsboys should keep the halfpence for themselves? Certain it is that the paper had a wide and speedy circulation, and though Stephen modestly refuses it a permanent place in the world of letters, it played a very important and effective part in Fawcett's candidature.

When the conflict was at its highest the inaugural lecture as Professor of Political Economy took place. Fawcett delivered the lecture at Cambridge in the morning, and the same evening was back in Brighton addressing a meeting.

Nomination Day.

On nomination day the candidates duly drove to the Town Hall. In the sixties this was an occasion for much rowdiness. The blind candidate did not shrink from rough contacts, and doubtless enjoyed the commotion as much as any. The varying notes in the discordant shouts of the mob told his sensitive ears every subtlety of friendly greeting or enmity. The rattle of pebbles against the window panes, or their thud as they struck a victim, the squelch of an ancient egg against the side of the carriage—all bore their message to the man from whom sight was withheld.

Political Eggs.

And the sense of smell brought him knowledge too—of the hot, unwashed crowd, of the dust-trampled road, of the stale vegetables and 'political eggs' that hurtled through the air. Every phase of the day's emotion was present to him and shared by him, thanks to his imagination, alertness and genial power of good fellowship.

The election took place on February 15.

Fawcett headed the poll in the early hours, when the working men voted, but he was finally defeated by one hundred and ninety-five by Moore, the Conservative candidate. Had the votes not been so split up by four candidates, the Liberal triumph would have been secured and Fawcett elected.

He took his defeat cheerfully, and indeed had some reason to be satisfied. He had done quite well enough for his success in the next election to seem positive.

In the autumn of the same year he again addressed meetings at Brighton, and made his best speech on Parliamentary Reform.

'Fawcett spoke of the honourable attitude of the working classes during the American War, and upon the reception of Garibaldi in London. They proved, he said, that the questions which really roused enthusiasm in the English people were those which appealed to their moral sentiments. He argued that something must be rotten if a man at 20s. a week had not as much interest in the peace and prosperity of the country as his neighbour with £10,000 a year. The sufferings inflicted by a war fall chiefly upon the poor; and any argument which implied that they should be rightfully excluded from the franchise as incompetent and indifferent, was an argument denoting a degraded and unwholesome state of feeling.'

The Tide of Freedom.

It is significant how Fawcett's whole nature rose to the wave of independence which was flooding the world. The emancipation of Italy, the freeing of the American slaves, and kindred struggles to give the lesser man a fair chance, found an echo in the policy which he championed for the helpless labouring classes. He was a lusty swimmer on this tide of freedom. He believed that working men were divided in their opinions as much as any other class, and that therefore, it was futile to fear that the rich vote would be killed by the poor. His attitude towards any proposal for reform of the franchise was: 'Do we think it will cause the various sections of opinion to be more independently and honestly represented?'

Mill thought well of Fawcett's speech on Parliamentary Reform, but he was opposed to his doctrine that workmen would not probably be united in their opinions. Mill felt that no matter how workmen might differ on other points, they would be united on whatever touched their class interests.

Back to Brighton.

The Brighton election was now at hand. At a great meeting held at the riding-school of the Pavilion, the two Liberal candidates, Mr. White, the sitting Liberal member, and Fawcett appeared, and resolutions in their favour were passed. Fawcett's father was also present and enthusiastically received. Fawcett placed his difficulties cheerfully before his audience. 'A Tory,' he said, 'had summed them up by saying that he would have to contend with £1500 from the Carlton, and a cartload of slander.'

The serious arguments against Fawcett were that he was a poor man, and that he was plotting the ruin of the tradesmen by his advocacy of co-operation. He frankly accepted both these charges, saying that he favoured co-operation as the best cure for poverty, and that he was certainly poor, having deliberately preferred the study of politics to money-making. Poverty, he said, did not weaken a man's influence in Parliament. Cobden, then recently dead, was a poor man, but he had 'vanquished a proud aristocracy and had given cheap bread to millions of his countrymen.' 'Every word uttered by Cobden in the House of Commons made its impression, whilst the words of millionaires might pass unnoticed.' Poverty would not destroy a man's influence in the House, if he were thoroughly qualified for his position, nor would it prevent his return by an independent constituency in spite of all ostentation of richer men.

In this case, Fawcett's optimism was justified, though Mammon had his usual good position in Brighton; candidates who could dispense champagne freely and spend money to help trade and politics were naturally preferred to candidates who were equipped solely with lofty principles and poverty. So it is much to the credit of the community that for at least a time it accepted higher things, and elected a blind member with high ideals and no money.

The Victor.

On the day of the election (July 12, 1865) 6492 out of 8661 electors polled, and the numbers were—White 3065; Fawcett 2665; Moore 2134.

At last Fawcett was an M.P., and at thirty-two had arrived at the goal towards which from boyhood he had set himself so unflinchingly. The letter which he wrote to his father of his first day in the House of Commons, deserves to be quoted in full.

'123 CAMBRIDGE STREET, WARWICK SQUARE,
LONDON, Feb. 1, 1866.

A Letter home.

'MY DEAR FATHER,—I have just returned from my first experience of the House of Commons. I went there early in the morning, and soon found that I should have no difficulty in finding my way about. I walked in with Tom Hughes about five minutes to two, and a most convenient seat close to the door was at once, as it were, conceded to me; and I have no doubt that it will always be considered my seat. Every one was most kind, and I was quite overwhelmed with congratulations. I am glad that my first visit is over, as I shall now feel perfect confidence that I shall be able to get on without any particular difficulty. The seat I have is as convenient a one as any in the House, and a capital place to speak from. I walked away from the House of Commons with Mill. He sits on the bench just above me, close to Bright. I sit next but one to Danby Seymour. White (his colleague for Brighton) is three or four places from me.

'Mother has indeed made a most wise selection in lodgings. They at present seem everything I could desire; the rooms are larger than I expected, and Mrs. Lark and the servant are most civil and obliging. This is everything in lodgings. I can walk to the House of Commons in exactly a quarter of an hour; this is not too far. Accept my best thanks for the hamper. Everything has arrived quite safely, and all the contents will prove most acceptable. We are going to have the fowl for dinner to-night at seven. I hope, now that I am so comfortably settled, some of you will often come to London. When am I to expect Maria? Give my kindest love to Mother and to her, and in great haste, to save post, believe me, dear Father, ever yours affectionately,

'Henry Fawcett.'

Parliamentary Arena.

When Fawcett was elected M.P. the great 'Pam' still led the Liberals, Radicals and Whigs, but he died before Parliament met. By the time of Fawcett's visit to the House described in the foregoing letter, Lord John Russell, the successor of Lord Palmerston as Prime Minister, had resigned the leadership of the Commons to Gladstone, who for a generation was to dominate English Liberalism. Bright, known to his supporters as the Tribune of the People, from his seat below the gangway, led the Radical wing. It was much strengthened by many new men, among whom John Stuart Mill was conspicuous. He represented Westminster, having experienced perhaps the most unique election in English politics. The Conservative opposition was led by Disraeli, known already, not only as a wearer of gorgeous waistcoats and a writer of brilliant political novels, but also for his strong and vivid personality. In the next few years he was to show his even more extraordinary gifts as a manipulator of Parliaments.

CHAPTER XVII

A PROPHETIC QUESTION IN PARLIAMENT

The Blind and Silent M.P.—His First Speech—Protecting Cattle, Neglecting Children—Industry earns Penury—Mill 'out.'

The Blind and Silent M.P.

Surrounded by these picturesque personages already so familiar to him, some by repute, and some by personal friendship, the blind M.P. quietly took his place. He had to learn the ways of the House, and, duly estimating the value of the unspoken word, said very little during his first Parliament.

His First Speech.

In view of his subsequent career, it is suggestive that Fawcett spoke in Parliament almost for the first time 'when he asked why the wages of certain letter-carriers had not been raised by the Post Office.' His first serious speech was in March 1866, in favour of the ill-fated Reform Bill brought in by Russell, and hailed by Bright with the doubtful welcome that half a loaf is better than no bread.

Fawcett in this speech repudiated indignantly the sneers at the working classes made by certain Whigs, and praised the fine political sense shown by them during the American War. He said that the problems of the future were the problems of capital and labour, and in these the working classes were most deeply interested and should directly affect the decisions to be made. He further maintained (in spite of the previously noted criticism of Mill) that the working classes would no more vote *en masse* than any other section of the community.

Where Fawcett sat.

As the gentle reader may know, in the House of Commons the long benches, upholstered in dark green leather, face one another in two raised tiers. There are no desks as in the American House of Representatives, and the men sit close together, the serried rows of faces making long lines of light against the dark background. Between them is the broad passage-way that leads up from the bar to the Speaker's chair, in front of which is set the great table on which many a minister's hand has hammered away his superabundant energy as his words made history. Fawcett sat on the lowest bench at the end farthest from the table. When he stood up to speak he was in all his long length in full view of the members who opposed him and of the leaders of his own party, who sat near the table on a bench that was continuous with his own.

The impression he made when speaking was of intense earnestness. His commanding presence and strongly marked individuality compelled attention. His voice was phenomenally clear, ranging from an almost nasal twang to tones of rare sweetness. His head was held very erect, every feature quick with intelligence saving the eyes shaded by the dark glasses, which gave a pathos to the face. The mouth was very mobile, sometimes trembling with eagerness for utterance, and with an underlying expression of wistfulness often routed by swift smiles. There was never anything cheap or theatrical about the man; he was simple, genuine, noble, and spoke fearlessly from his big heart, pleading the cause of the poor and the oppressed.

The Reform Bill was withdrawn, and at the end of the summer the Liberals resigned office. There was no general election, and the next year Disraeli from the Government benches faced a House in which the majority were in opposition.

Tea-Room Party.

During the winter there had been so much demonstration of public feeling that the Conservatives had to bring in a Reform Bill of their own. Their Bill appeared to be generous, but was hedged about with many provisoes and exceptions. Gladstone wished his followers to vote against it on the ground that it was hopelessly bad, and Bright agreed with this policy. But some Radicals, among whom was Fawcett, considered that to vote against any Reform Bill was retrograde, and they declined to follow Gladstone's lead. These men were known as the Tea-Room Party, as they plotted their rebellion from that comfortable retreat within the recesses of the Parliamentary buildings. They held out, in spite of the reproach that they were showing more confidence in their opponents than in their own leaders, and contended that to vote against any Reform was to put themselves in a false position. A deputation of five, of which one was Fawcett, waited on Gladstone to give their views. Fawcett was distressed at this early necessity of opposing his chief, and often spoke with admiration of Gladstone's earnestness and ability. The Tea-Room party won their way, and Disraeli's Bill passed, but the Liberals and Radicals so altered it that it became a more democratic bill than the one the Tory leader and his party had opposed the previous session.

It was during these debates that Fawcett both spoke and voted in favour of Mill's amendment to admit women to the franchise.

Protecting Cattle, neglecting Children.

During his first Parliament he made himself felt as an ardent and determined Radical. He made various proposals to help his poor friends the labourers in the agricultural districts, and spoke forcibly on 'the interest taken in the cattle-plague, by some members, and the want of interest in the more terrible plague which was ruining thousands of the constituents of the same gentlemen.'

He urged the extension of the Factory Acts to agricultural labourers, and complained that these Acts had been opposed by the rich on the 'paltry or cold-hearted plea that they would interfere with industry; as if it were the mission of a great nation simply to produce bales of goods and to swell exports and imports, even at the cost of sacrificing the health and blighting the minds of the young!'

It was in order to promote the prosperity of all classes that Fawcett longed for a truly national and representative Parliament. He had no sympathy with those who thought it necessary to 'stem the tide of democracy.'

He was also eager to make it more possible for poor men to enter Parliament, and urged a reform that is still being agitated—that the expenses of the returning officers at elections should be paid by the State. 'It was impossible,' he said, 'to exaggerate the mischief of thus shutting out the ablest men from political life.' This reform was urged many times and in different Parliaments by Fawcett, but in spite of his tenacity he did not succeed in carrying it through.

Already he had entered into that discussion of Indian affairs which was to open up such a noble chapter in his life. He had also done good service in committee on the Bill for University Reform. An impression on the House had been made by his honest zeal, and though he had been perhaps a little too radical for his party leader, his Radical supporters could find no reason for dissatisfaction with him. For all time the chimæra that his blindness would prove an obstacle to his remarkable efficiency had disappeared.

General Election of 1868.

Parliament was dissolved in 1868, and a general election took place in the summer. Part of the constituency of Brighton longed for a rich representative, and as one of his opponents was popular and kept a yacht, Fawcett's struggle for re-election was sharply fought, and he came out with no more than a respectable majority.

Gladstone was re-elected, but all the working-class candidates were defeated. This distressed Fawcett greatly. His friendships with many working men, and his knowledge of their fitness to represent their fellows, made him appreciate the real loss this meant to the country.

Professor Cairnes of Dublin had first met Fawcett in the long ago days of the British Association Meeting at Aberdeen. He was a political economist of much distinction, but had become a helpless invalid, and lived for years in great suffering. Fawcett had much affection for him, and neglected no opportunity to run down to his friend's house at Blackheath, taking to the sufferer by his own vitality, and high, mirth-loving spirits, encouragement, new life and energy. Lord Courtney completed the congenial and closely united trio, and Fawcett's public action was often the result of much careful discussion with the other two.

The following letter, written during these elections to his invalid friend, shows much of Fawcett's feeling at the time.

The Condition of Affairs.

'I begin to be very confident that Gladstone will obtain a great majority. The

Irish Church would have been a good cry to have appealed to the old constituencies on, but working men neither care about the Irish Church nor any other Church. The election, though satisfactory in a party sense, will, I fear, return a House scarcely superior in character to the last. Few good new men are coming out, and more over-rich manufacturers and iron-masters are standing than ever. Before the next general election after the coming one, the working men will have felt their power and will have learnt, perhaps by bitter experience, that Liberals do not all belong to the same species; in fact a consummate naturalist, like Darwin, would classify Mill and Harvey Lewis as belonging to different and well-defined genera. Something must be done immediately Parliament meets to check election expenses. When last I saw you in Dover Street, I little thought that late that evening the Government would give notice of reversing the clause I passed for throwing necessary election expenses on the rates.

'The shabby tactics of Disraeli have done much to make the country favour the clause. If I am returned I shall embody the clause in a bill and introduce it the first night of the session. I have had no news about Westminster since leaving London, but I cling to the conviction that Mill is safe. I spent a day at Brighton about a fortnight since, and everything there looks as promising as possible. Did you read Hooker's address to the British Association? Some portions of it were most masterly; the *Spectator* is, I think, just in its criticism of his sweeping hostility to all metaphysics.

Industry earns Penury.

When the next essay is written on peasant proprietors, the £26,000,000 which have been subscribed in cash, a great portion of it by French peasants, to the recent loan, will provide a strong argument in favour of cultivation by the owner. I am staying in the midst of what is considered to be one of the most prosperous agricultural districts of England. It would be almost impossible to find a labourer who had saved a sovereign, and not one in a thousand of these labourers will save enough to keep him from the poor rates when old age compels him to cease work. Yet nine Englishmen out of ten think that it is in agriculture that we show our great superiority to the French.'

Cairnes replies with an interesting letter of warm congratulations, in which he deplores bitterly the defeat as candidate for the Liberal party of that 'exemplar of far-seeing statesmanship, commanding views, and lofty moral purpose,' Mill, and adds, 'How the enemies of truth and light will blaspheme!'

Mill 'out.'

Fawcett's reply to Cairnes' letter gives a vivid idea of the condition of politics. He writes in December 1868, 'You and I feel alike about the rejection of Mill. Those who have watched him in the House of Commons can perhaps fully realise the injury which his rejection has inflicted on English politics. He diffused a certain moral atmosphere over an assembly whose average tone is certainly not high. A letter which I received from Mill yesterday confirms me in the belief I have long entertained, that Parliament involved to him a most severe personal sacrifice. He speaks almost with enthusiastic joy of being restored to freedom, and he is evidently supremely happy in the prospect of being able to work uninterruptedly. Still I am sure his sense of public duty is so high that he would at once accept a seat if one were offered to him. The working men know what a friend he is of theirs, and I believe they are determined to return him the first time a good opportunity offers. The Liberal majority at the general election is of course eminently satisfactory, but there is much in the constitution of the present House which is very disappointing. Intellectually it is inferior to the last, and wealthy uneducated manufacturers and merchants are more predominant than ever. Mill always predicted that this would be the case, thinking that the new voters would require two or three years to understand the power which had been given to them.

The third Brighton contest.

'I had a hard fight at Brighton. Not only was there disunion in my own party, got up by a small section, who thought I did not spend enough money in the town, but the Tory who opposed me was very rich, and all that wealth could do against me was done.

'My success was peculiarly satisfactory, because it was obtained without a paid agent or a paid canvasser; and we never held even a meeting at a public house.

'I quite agree with you that the present Government will have to be most narrowly watched with regard to what they do upon education and the land question.'

His ever-increasing responsibilities exhilarated Fawcett, and his friendships increased in proportion; he was always accumulating relays of young friends who filled up the sad gaps caused by death. If he had lived to be a Methuselah he would have died regretted by troops of young folks. He and his wife were now much sought after, and they much enjoyed festivities together. Mrs. Fawcett was frequently amused by her husband's delight in gossip and his irrepressible boyishness.

One evening, at the house of a friend, Fawcett met another M.P. They immediately retired together to a remote corner of the room, where they discussed in low and earnest voices. Mrs. Fawcett, thinking that they were debating matters of State, was much surprised when she happened to pass near them to hear Fawcett asking eagerly, 'Was it her fault or his fault?'

Roller Skating.

On another occasion, shortly after skating on rollers was introduced, Mrs. Fawcett went to a rink, and as she came in was told that a most extraordinary thing was going on—there was a blind man trying roller-skating. It was her husband, whizzing round delightedly. Fawcett was having a royal time, darting like a huge swallow in swift circles about the skating rink. He revelled in the motion and the exercise, which put him into a fine glow. The merry noise of many little wooden wheels rolling smoothly over the polished floor—the lifting and stumbling of awkward feet, and the skilful glide of the good skaters gave him a happy consciousness of the gay revolving spectacle through which he winged his way.

CHAPTER XVIII

GLADSTONE PRIME MINISTER

Opposition to Gladstone—'The most Thorough Radical Member in
the House'—Growing Dissatisfaction with the Government—The
Irish Universities Bill—Helping to Defeat his own Party.

Gladstone and Fawcett.

In the new Parliament Gladstone became Prime Minister for the first time.
Fawcett had much appreciation of his leader's wonderful powers, of his ability
as a financier, of his sincerity as a reformer, and of his right to the support of the
Liberal party.

But the ramifications, subtleties and luminosities of Gladstone's marvellous
intellect and culture were a closed book to Fawcett's downright, strong, unimag-
inative and limited mind, limited in a sense by its very excellencies, its honesties,
its insistence on the real, the well proved, his willingness to consider the workable
problem only, rejecting all inquiries which savoured of the visionary, the philo-
sophic, or the purely æsthetic. Whatever Fawcett's mind was willing to dally with
or to assimilate must have the qualities of serviceableness and a certain homespun simplicity. Culture for its own sake, the higher flights of the imagination, and
struggles to pierce the veil of the unknown seemed to him a sentimental waste of
good time which could better be spent on real work or good play.

A Difference in Temperaments.

The great flights which Gladstone's intellect revelled in, his delight in ancient
as well as in the most recent philosophy, seemed as amusing and unnecessary to
Fawcett as it was to him profitless and extravagant.

In their entirely divergent points of view we must recognise the cause of much
of the later incompatibility of these two temperaments which really never understood each other, and had not the power to meet on a truly common footing.

The Bills of 1869.

In the session of 1869 they struck fire more than once. The Bill for removing Religious Tests at the Universities did not satisfy Fawcett, and he also much
disapproved of the financial arrangements in the Bill for disestablishing the Irish
Church. The Education Bill pleased him as little. The phrase 'We must educate

our masters' represented the feeling of many in regard to the newly enfranchised labour. To them education was a desperate safeguard against a necessary evil. To Fawcett it was the beautiful and logical outcome of a simple act of justice. The Education Bill of 1870 was hampered by conflicting religious difficulties, and the resultant law was a compromise little to Fawcett's liking.

Fawcett's position in Parliament had now become strong and unique. A contemporary writes of him as 'the most thorough Radical now in the House.' He was regarded as a leader of the extreme party.

A Radical of the Radicals.

As a critic of the Government he was ruthless and reckless, like a mighty woodman hacking mercilessly at ill-grown timber. There was ample reason for his dissatisfaction, as he emphatically proved to a crowded meeting at Brighton.

He began by telling a story to which he often referred. Some old-fashioned Liberal had told him that after two hours' reflection he and his friends had been unable to answer the question, what there was for the Liberal party to do. Fawcett said that he had enlightened his friend in the course of a short stroll, and he now proceeded to enlighten his constituents. He began by insisting upon the shortcomings of the previous sessions. The Irish Church had been disestablished, but at the cost of a bribe of £7,000,000. The praise bestowed upon the Education Act was, as often happened, one more proof that it was 'a feeble and timorous compromise.' Time had been wasted in 'squabbling over a paltry religious difficulty,' which had been handed over to the local authorities instead of finally settled by Parliament. The University Tests had been only half settled. The Ballot Bill was a good measure, yet it left the most serious difficulty of election expenses inadequately treated. 'We had therefore still to make up leeway; but above all we had to introduce new ideas.' In this last sentence he emphasised the paralysis of progress which had so long crippled the advance of England. New cures, new methods, new energy, were what this young politician had craved from the first of his co-workers.

New Ideas.

Full of life and enthusiasm, the blind youth abounded in plans to make the world happier and saner. It should have no rest till his thoughts had become beneficient law. He prodded those sedate Whiggish gentlemen who formed so large a part of the Liberal majority on the importance of a fair minority representation. He cried out that there must be 'no more hereditary legislation, and that the House of Lords needed reform.' He held before them abuses connected with the Poor Laws, and the horrible fact that in England one in every twenty of their fellows was then a pauper.

Being disagreeable.

The party whips and organisers used to say that whatever was proposed, Fawcett would say something disagreeable. Fawcett did, in fact, say the 'most disagreeable' thing pretty often, because nothing can be so disagreeable as an opposition based upon the very principle of which the party claims a special monopoly.

Fawcett's increasing dissatisfaction with the Government was strongly set forth in an article in the *Fortnightly Review* of 1871 'On the Present Position of the Government.'

It was a vigorous criticism of the ministry. While giving them credit for what they had done, he contended that the reforms that had been attempted were but half-heartedly done, and had not met the evils they were supposed to overcome. He mentioned many of the questions we have already referred to, but he also spoke of two others that will be discussed more fully in later chapters. He complained that the Government had done its utmost to promote the enclosure of English commons, and that Indian Finance had been dismissed by the Cabinet with fifteen minutes' discussion.

He forestalled the rejoinder that the Government was not to be expected to satisfy the extreme Radicals, by claiming that it did not even keep up with the main body of its supporters. It was enormously pleased with itself when it, 'after much curious twisting, and many a dubious halt, decided to accept a principle which, years before, had been endorsed at a hundred provincial meetings.'

He felt that while Government could have kept the enthusiasm of its supporters by following out a simple, strong policy, it had injured itself and disgusted them, not by going too far, but by shilly-shallying, compromising, and equivocating. This frankness hurt Fawcett's position with the strong supporters of the Government, and he was looked on as its enemy, so that the Government Whips did not even send him the usual notices.

The Irish University Bill.

Then came the last great battle of that Parliament, in which Fawcett was to play so dramatic a part. Trinity College, Dublin, was a Protestant university financed by the State. Liberals were eager to remove the religious tests which prevented Catholics from enjoying the emoluments of the college. This proposal had Fawcett's enthusiastic sympathy. His standpoint in dealing with these questions can best be shown by a comment he once made on Mill's book on *Liberty*.

'As I was reading Mill's *Liberty*—perhaps the greatest work of our greatest living writer—as I read his noble, I might almost say his holy ideas, I thought to myself, if every one in my country could and would do his work, how infinitely happier would the nation be! How much less desirous should we be to wrangle about petty religious differences! How much less of the energy of the nation would be wasted in contemptible quarrels about creeds and formularies; and how much more powerful should we be as a nation to achieve works of good, when, as this work would teach us to be, we were firmly bound together by the bonds of a wise toleration.'

Fawcett resented any narrow sectarian rules, and, though never irreligious, was out of sympathy with ceremonial and dogmatic detail.

He himself really lived according to the creed that 'the world was his country, and to do good his religion.' He had probably little true understanding of the depth of feeling that can be aroused by differences of creed and church. All men were alike to him, the Catholic, the Jew, or the Agnostic; and for Ireland as well as for England he fought for absolute equality of privilege for all.

Even in his first Parliament, Fawcett had urged the removal of religious tests in Dublin, and had continued to do so in the various sessions that followed. His friend, Professor Cairnes, and he would discuss the matter. Fawcett studied it very thoroughly and pressed this reform incessantly. At last in 1873, when he had again brought in a Bill for abolishing tests and for certain other changes, he agreed to withdraw it in favour of a Government Bill if this latter should seem to him sufficiently satisfactory.

Gladstone's Speech.

The Government measure was introduced by Gladstone in a speech so persuasive that Fawcett said that 'if the decision could have taken place whilst the House was still under its spell, the Bill would have been almost unanimously carried.' But, after a careful examination, Fawcett found it impossible to give it his support. He was, however, much moved by Gladstone's speech, and afterwards congratulated him most heartily on his eloquence. Gladstone's eagle eye glanced at him with a slight air of reproach as he replied, 'I could have wished that it had proved more persuasive, sir.'

The scheme of the Bill was very complicated. The various colleges in Ireland, Catholic and Protestant, were to be combined into one university. Instruction in subjects likely to be controversial was to be limited to the colleges themselves. These subjects were theology, moral philosophy, and modern history. On these the university Professors were not to lecture, nor was the university to examine in them. 'Gagging clauses' Fawcett called these, and made against them the ablest speech of his life. He lifted the debate out of the level plain of Parliamentary commonplace, and almost savagely closed with the weak arguments of his antagonists, and vanquished them. He contended that the proposed regulations would make 'the treatment of all subjects, even political economy, for example, hopeless' and would seem a Government sanction of any criticism advanced by any religious authority. The separate colleges, each with their separate religious control, would perpetuate and deepen the bitter religious quarrels from which Ireland had suffered so long.

When Fawcett felt that it was his mission to drive home an idea, so that it would penetrate and permeate unforgettably the minds of his auditors, he set out deliberately to pierce like a steel drill the rock of opposition. His relentless facts bored a hole in the wall of antagonism, which he then tried to fill with the dynamite of action. When embittered and roused to righteous anger, his words were like blows. Often his enemies gave in from sheer weariness, because their reasons were too black and blue to fight his logic any longer.

HENRY FAWCETT

Fawcett's Bill passed.

Opposition seemed only to feed his triple flame of courage, resourcefulness, and energy. The ministers received but lukewarm support, and were unable to withstand Fawcett's onslaught. The Bill was defeated in division, and immediately Fawcett brought in his own measure. The Government agreed to support it if all changes but those abolishing religious tests were omitted. Fawcett consented, and at last, after many years struggle, his Bill became law.

This defeat of the Ministry by some of its own supporters was one of the main causes which brought about its fall. Fawcett had dared that courageous thing, to wreck his own party rather than consent to a Bill of which he disapproved. He did more, for Gladstone retired from the leadership shortly after this, and largely because of the weak support of members of his own party. It says well for both that the two men worked together later on several occasions.

Fawcett was never a party man in the sense of submitting his judgment to the policy of his leaders; but he kept their respect, for his honesty could not be questioned, and when he turned and rent his own party, it was because he felt it lacked that Liberalism for which it stood. The fact that his action was likely to stand in the way of his chance of office was a consideration which it would never occur to him to entertain. He desired office, but as a better means of serving the people; if office could not mean that to him, it meant nothing.

SAVING THE PEOPLE'S PLAY-GROUNDS

'Trust thyself: every heart vibrates to the iron string. God will not have His work made manifest by cowards.'

—Emerson.

CHAPTER XIX

THE STOLEN COMMONS

The Disappearance of the English Playgrounds and Commons—Fawcett's first Protest—The Annual Enclosure Bill stopped by his energetic Action.

A Countryman to the Rescue.

Fawcett used to say that there was no part of his public work on which he looked with so much unalloyed satisfaction as on his work for the commons. Perhaps a few words show what a complicated question he had to deal with, and how great the need was for the strong and courageous action which he took in this matter.

He would see the urgency as only those could see it whose knowledge of country life and country ways was drawn from the farming and labouring classes. He kept true to his early lessons and did not allow his path to be deviated by the many side issues in which these questions were involved.

Common Lands.

From the earliest times there had been in every parish in England a large tract of land held in common. Part of it was cultivated jointly by the villagers and part of it was kept as open common land, and all parishioners had the right to feed their beasts there, and to cut wood or furze, and similar privileges.

This gave much independence to the simpler folk and added to their resources and comforts, but it also made it impossible to farm the common lands by more modern and more productive methods. So there arose a movement for enclosing these lands and dividing them up among the different village inhabitants, to become their own individual property. As regards the lands farmed jointly, this course had many advantages provided that the distribution was made fairly. But when it came to the commons proper, the benefit was much more doubtful even from a wealth-giving point of view. As to the non-economic value of a common—its value as an open place for recreation and health-giving—this only began to be realised as the commons became few.

Fawcett, in his first professional lectures (1864), mentions the evils arising from enclosures.

No room for the Cow and the Pig.

'He declared, from his own knowledge of the agricultural labourer, that cottagers could no longer keep a cow, a pig, or poultry; that the village greens had become extinct, and that the turnpike road was too often the only playground for the village children.

'He doubted whether the enclosure of commons, involving the breaking up of pastures, had, in point of fact, permanently increased the wealth of the country; but the wealth in any case was dearly purchased if purchased by a diminution of the labourers' comforts. The compensation paid to the poor commoner had generally been spent by the first receiver, whilst his descendants were permanently deprived of many of the little advantages which might have helped to eke out their scanty resources.'

The procedure whereby a common was enclosed was one that dealt very hardly on the poorer folk, and made it very difficult, if not impossible, for them to make their objections felt. The matter went before the Enclosure Commissioners, and they every year presented a Bill to Parliament recommending such enclosures as they had at that time approved. The Bill would be passed almost without investigation, as part of the routine work of Parliament.

Fawcett appreciated from a child the blessings of open free tracts for fresh air and fun. He watched with distress and indignation the rights of the people to their woods and open spaces being put aside, their commons seized and fenced off, their forests appropriated and their venerable trees cut down—and all this without protest, nay by the consent of a Government which undertook to be the guardian of the people's interests. Their historic right in Epping Forest, Hampstead Heath, and many other places were ignored in mean schemes for appropriating the land and raising paltry sums by selling it as farm or building land, or by marketing the timber. Fawcett might have chanted in his sonorous voice the following apt and classic verse:

> The law locks up the man or woman
> Who steals the goose from off the common,
> But lets the greater villain loose
> Who steals the common from the goose.

Battle of Wisley Common.

The annual enclosure Bill, introduced in 1869, submitted over six thousand acres for enclosure, of which only three acres were to be reserved for the public. In this area was included the beautiful common of Wisley. It chanced that a resident near Wisley, who was a member of Parliament, strongly objected to enclosures, and to this one in particular, and he drew the attention of the House to the case. The Minister in charge of the Bill agreed to withdraw Wisley and refer it to a select committee, but said, at the same time, that it would be obviously unfair to stop unopposed enclosures, and he proposed to proceed with the rest of the Bill.

Fawcett, who joined in the debate, was made a member of this committee, but his interest and energy went further. The Wisley case had fixed his attention on the nature of the Bill itself, and he saw that there was every reason to suppose that similar but unnoticed abuses were occurring. The Bill had almost reached its final stage in the House of Commons, but Fawcett was not to be stopped. He gave notice that 'upon the third reading he should move for a recommittal of the Bill in order that a better provision might be made for allotments.' This motion created a great outcry. Why this interference? Parliament had been getting along most harmoniously with the Enclosure Commission. Why change this comfortable order of things and create delay and inconvenience to those interested in making enclosures? Fawcett had a hearty contempt for this comfort and convenience at the expense of the poor. He continued his efforts to stop the passage of the Bill.

Outwitting the Whips.

The Government Whips, whose business it is to get business done, tried to evade Fawcett's opposition by arranging for the Bill to be discussed at awkward times. They arranged for it to come on half an hour after midnight, after the main business of the sitting was finished. Night after night it would be put off on one excuse or another, and Fawcett and the small band of friends who supported him would wait in vain. None the less, they took turns and tried to be always on guard, for they knew that their absence would be the signal for hurrying the Bill through. Fawcett used to tell this story with glee: one night, as he had a very bad cold, he sent a message to the Whips asking to have the motion postponed again as had been so frequently done before. He had no answer, but trusting that his request would be granted, he went home to bed. A friend who dropped in to see him suggested that it would be unwise to relax guard even for the night. Fawcett thereupon hurled on his clothes and arrived to find the House about to pass the obnoxious Bill.

The wily Whip started 'like a guilty thing surprised,' and admitted good-naturedly the failure of his tactics, and gave a formal undertaking to defer the Bill then and to arrange for it to be brought on later at a reasonable hour. Then, at last, Fawcett moved his resolution, dwelt upon the injustice to the labourer, of the absurdly small reservations for public allotments, protested at the attitude of the speakers for the Government, who shirked all responsibility beyond confirming the action of the commissioners. On his motion a committee was appointed to consider the working of the present system, and the expediency of better provision for recreation and allotment grounds.

Fawcett opposes the traditional.

In committee Fawcett opposed the existing system. The Enclosure Commissioners and their supporters were content with the doctrine, that 'the final cause of an enclosure commission is naturally to enclose,' and considered it advantageous to get rid of common rights which obstructed a more profitable employment of the land. Surely, they claimed, it is a hardship to prevent the owners of any piece of property from distributing their various rights on terms upon which they all agree. Fawcett argued that the agreement was illusory. Country gentlemen and farmers had looked after themselves, but the cottager had been put off with some trifle, spent as soon as received.

Withypool Parish Clerk.

Fawcett was particularly delighted with the evidence given by Mr. J. Reed, parish clerk of Withypool. When asked how far people would have to go for an open space, the witness replied, 'They could not find one for miles except they did go on the common.' 'Is there no common within reach of an ordinary walk?' 'No, he would not want any more recreation by the time he came to any other common. The people say they will be as badly off as in a town.' 'Are there no fields where they can walk?' 'Yes, they can trespass, if they like that.'

The committee's report, after vigorous discussion, accepted the chief principles advocated by Fawcett; 'Parliamentary scrutiny was to become real and searching.' Bills should be more carefully prepared in future. It was even admitted to be questionable whether enclosures were always beneficial.

Thus was a first great battle won for the safety of the commons. Others had felt the wrong as well as Fawcett, and supported him loyally, but it was his bulldog tenacity and his doing the disagreeable thing that finally throttled the Annual Enclosures Bill and stopped the mechanical process by which so many harmful enclosures were made.

Sir Robert Hunter.

Fawcett made a notable speech against this Bill. The late Sir Robert Hunter, who saw much of Fawcett at this time, says: 'Mr. Fawcett's memory was very remarkable, apart from the recognition of voices. I remember an instance of this which struck me very much. He was making a stand against the enclosure of rural commons; the question arose whether certain enclosures which had been commenced should be carried out or abandoned. There were some twenty or thirty cases, and Mr. Fawcett in a speech to the House of Commons gave figured details of each case, the whole area of each common, the extent of the allotments for fields, for gardens and a host of other particulars.

The Style for the House.

But all his friends were not so appreciative. Lord Courtney tells how Fawcett on one occasion took a Liverpool man of little humour down to Cambridge for the Christmas dinner. In return for his hospitality the guest rewarded Fawcett by fearless and supercilious criticism of his method of speaking, saying, 'Fawcett, you haven't got the style for the House of Commons!' Fawcett accepted the criticism in good part and his friend undertook to show how to speak, rising to his feet and gesticulating dramatically and making himself greatly absurd. Fawcett, after a little good-natured listening, excused himself on the plea of an engagement, saying, 'Thanks ever so much. Edward,' indicating his guide, who was present, 'is a first-rate reporter, and will tell me the rest of your speech when I return.' With which he flung gaily out of the room, leaving his instructor agape.

Perhaps he had fled to go skating. His enthusiasm for this sport was unquenchable. A Cambridge friend of those days writes:

'Fawcett insisted that skating was best on the first day of a thaw. He would come to my room, calling in his cheerful, loud voice, "Hullo, are you going skating?" More than once I argued with him without avail that it was dangerous to skate when the ice was thinning. He was deaf to all reason, and would haul me out on the river, where he would skate ankle deep in water. Well I remember my alarm once when I saw him—he was heading full tilt towards a big hole. I shouted to him to steer clear of it, myself horrified at his imminent danger. When he barely escaped the opening he called out cheerily. "Oh, don't worry, it will be all right!" Shod with his skates he was absolutely without fear.'

CHAPTER XX

THE FIGHT FOR THE FOREST

The Commons Preservation Society—The saving of Epping Forest—
The Queen's Rights—The Lords of the Manors' Rights—The People's Rights.

A society had been founded in 1865, called the Commons Preservation Society, which had for object to defend the public rights in the commons round London. Two years later Fawcett joined their committee and attended their meetings
sedulously. One of his first actions was to recommend that the sphere of their
operations be extended to the country at large.

Epping Forest.

He found them busy in the effort to save Epping Forest, which stretches some
ten to thirty miles to the north-east of the city. It is one of the most beautiful forests
of England. Old trees stand there that in their youth witnessed the hunting of Sax-
on kings. Epping Forest was for many centuries a favourite royal hunting-ground.
Up to the time of Charles II., kings followed the deer there in person. But after that
time the Crown no longer protected the game or looked after the woodlands, and
the district became waste land—subject only to certain rather vague rights of the
Crown, of the local lords of the manors, and of the commoners.

In the nineteenth century the Crown thought to turn an honest penny out of
Epping. It sold its forestal rights over some four thousand acres, about half the
area of the forest, to the neighbouring lords of the manors at an average price of
£5 an acre. These gentlemen now began gaily to enclose the land. The commoners
were few and powerless, and the lords of the manors professed to have compensated them or received their consent, where they did not ignore them altogether. One landowner calmly ploughed up three hundred acres without consent of
Crown or commons.

Prison for tree lopping.

But though much of the forest was lost in some places, in others it was successfully defended. For four years that part of the forest that is within the Manor
of Loughton was saved by the courage and public spirit of a labourer named Willingdale. By immemorial custom the men of that parish had the right of tree-lop-
ping, and on St. Martin's Eve at midnight they used to meet and go into the forest,
cut wood, and drag it to their homes. When the lord of this manor, who was also

the rector of the parish, enclosed thirteen hundred acres, Willingdale and his two sons, on the St. Martin's Eve following, broke through the fencing and lopped and carried away their wood. For this assertion of their rights they were summoned before the local justices and sentenced to two months' hard labour.

The sentence roused great indignation in East London. The Commons Preservation Society took up the matter, and a fund was raised to fight the case in the law-courts on behalf of Willingdale.

Willingdale himself had a hard time. Unless he continued to live in Loughton he had no right to bring his suit, but he could get no employment there, and was forced to accept a pension from the Commons Preservation Society. Even then he found it difficult to get a lodging in the village. He was more than once offered big bribes of money if he would abandon his suit. One son died in prison, and he himself died in 1870, but his pluck had saved the forest long enough for others to be found to take up the fight.

It was during this litigation that Fawcett became actively interested in the case. He appeared as one of a deputation from the Commons Preservation Society to the Chancellor of the Exchequer, and shared in the severe rebuke which that gentleman administered to the deputation.

Royal Rights made People's Rights.

This reception was enough in itself to set Fawcett to work. He proposed to move forthwith an address to the Queen, urging that the Crown rights might be defended, and by this means the forest kept free for the recreation of the people. He felt that a clear statement of a sane and popular principle would force the Liberal party to choose a definite course as champion either of popular rights or private interests.

In his determination to bring the whole matter thus before the public and challenge the Government policy, Fawcett stood quite alone. The best friends of the movement begged him to desist, believing he was inviting defeat, and would thus injure the cause, but he had a firmer belief in the strength of public opinion. It was another proof of that far-sighted independence of judgment which his fellow-workers learned so heartily to respect.

His influence on his friends deepened year by year. His personality is perhaps most felt in the strong impression he made on them. Professor Stewart, also an M.P., tells of Fawcett: 'He sat at times when we came to tell him things in his easy-chair with his hands holding the elbows of it, his face towards us, his lips a little parted, his whole physiognomy lit up with intelligence and interest, his mind evidently drawing before itself the picture of which we spoke, and the smile that was on his features playing even to his broad brow. Or again, when animated with his own clear mental vision, his whole frame eloquent, he spoke strong, incisive, direct words, looking through my very soul with his empty eyes.'

A friendly Cabby.

He very rarely went about alone, but the late Sir Robert Hunter told of once journeying to London with him one evening. 'When we arrived at Waterloo, Fawcett asked me to put him into a cab, and refused to let me go with him, shouting "Good-bye" merrily as he drove off into the night. Notwithstanding his fearlessness he seemed to me so helpless, this blind giant all alone in a cab in London, utterly at the mercy of the cabman.' But he had friends among the cabmen too, for once when he turned to pay a cabby his fare, the man utterly refused it with 'No, Mr. Fawcett, no, sir. You have done too much for the working man.'

When his motion came on in the House, he reviewed the whole question of Epping Forest and showed the value of the Crown rights as a protection of the people's rights. He stated that the Crown had sold its rights on four thousand acres for £18,603, 16s. 2d., so small an amount as to be negligible to the Chancellor of the Exchequer, and a healthful means of enjoyment for the people had been destroyed. Ten times the sum might have been saved by abolishing a sinecure office, such as the Lord Privy Seal. This last a truly Fawcettian fling.

Deer, yes. Picnickers, no!

The principal argument which he had to meet now was that 'the forest rights were relics of feudalism; they were useful to keep up deer for the royal hunting. Now that the Queen did not want to hunt it would be unfair to keep them up for a different purpose.' A man may not put up a fence to keep out the Queen's deer, but he may put it up to restrain a picnic party of her subjects. The Queen might not make over her rights to the public, but must resign them to the lords of the manors. Fawcett (taking, I fear, a real and humorous satisfaction in his reply) answered, 'If a right ceased when the original purpose became obsolete, what would become of the lord of the manor? He had ceased to discharge any duties; should he cease to have any rights?'

Fawcett's motion was strongly supported. Mr. Gladstone showed a wider appreciation of the significance of the problem than other members of his Government. He conceded that Fawcett had demonstrated that it was the duty of Government to take up the question, and as the champions of the people to secure whatever was practical. He proposed a modification, accepted by Fawcett, and the motion was passed.

This was a great triumph, but entire success was not yet assured. Government endorsed the policy of the Commons Preservation Society. The Prime Minister recognised that Fawcett's road was the right one to travel, but there were still many enemies who were to be won over to an appreciation of the people's rights. A compromise was proposed which seemed quite inadequate to the society. But the Government introduced a Bill on the lines of this so-called compromise which would have enclosed nearly all the forest and have left, perhaps, six hundred acres in various scattered plots to be reserved for public use.

An inept Proposal.

At once Fawcett gave notice of moving the rejection of this inept document. For this and other technical reasons the Bill was dropped. But even its short life had shown its infirmities to such a degree that Government was too wise to let it reappear.

High Beach.

The next year, 1871, the Commons Preservation Society was stirred to immediate action by a new danger. Notice was given that the most beautiful of the ancient trees in Epping, those of High Beach, were to be felled! High Beach was a part of the forest in which there were no Crown rights. The timber belonged to the lords of the manors and the rights of the public seemed difficult to ascertain. The Commons Preservation Society sat in committee, and Fawcett suggested that a motion should be proposed in the House of Commons desiring that measures should be taken for keeping open those parts of the forest which had not been enclosed by consent of the Crown, or by legal authority. This ingenious phrasing, for all its complicated appearance, would have the simple and satisfactory effect of saving Epping Forest until such time as the House of Commons legislated further on the subject. Fawcett suggested that this motion should be brought forward by Mr. Cowper Temple, who, on account of his previous services and his less extreme views, was much better qualified to press the matter than himself. This was like Fawcett, thorough and direct, standing back to give another his place whenever it meant better service.

Government opposed this resolution with all its force, but so strongly had the public feeling been roused that it was defeated by a majority of one hundred and one.

The Hunting-ground of Kings.

Later in the session the Government appointed a Royal Commission. And then the City of London found out that it also had forestal rights, and took the matter into the law-courts. For eleven weary years more the battle went on.

Five thousand acres secured for the People.

It was not till 1882 that Queen Victoria went in person to Epping Forest to hand over five thousand acres of the old hunting-ground of her ancestors to the people of England. But the critical time had been in those first years before the public conscience was roused. And in those years Fawcett's persistence had made the after-work possible.

By his brave common sense, and lucid justice and eloquence, Fawcett had won this great battle for the people for all time. In his article in the *Fortnightly*, the following November, he says: 'The few remaining commons are the only places where the people, except by sufferance, can leave the beaten pathway or the frequented high road.' 'And yet this Government, so grand in its popular professions, so strong in its hustings denunciations of those who would divorce the people from the soil, used the whole weight of official influence to enclose the few commons that were left.' 'so anxious were they to pursue this policy of depriving the public and the poor of their commons that night after night the House was kept sitting to two or three o'clock in the morning in order to pass an Enclosure Bill,' 'and the Ministry, apparently willing to risk something more than reputation in the cause, were disastrously defeated by those who were anxious to preserve Epping Forest.'

The Ministry had come to stigmatise him as 'impracticable.' Yet the course which he obliged them against their will to follow was of vital importance to the country, and it seems as if the 'impracticable' Fawcett, the blind Don Quixote, had not tilted in vain at his opponents.

CHAPTER XXI

FOR THE PEOPLE'S WOODS AND STREAMS

Saving the Forests—'The monstrous Nation'—Walking with Lord Morley—The Boat Race—Safeguarding the Rivers.

The shearing of a Statesman.

Fawcett had the knack of saving time and getting the most out of it. One spring day when he was going to pay a promised visit, absent-mindedly he put his hand to his hair, which he found rather long. Discovering that he had five minutes to spare, he shouted in his cheerful loud voice to the cabby through the opening in the roof of the hansom: 'stop at the first hairdresser's shop.' Arrived there he sprang out quickly and rushed in to the barber, exclaiming as he whizzed past him: 'Cut off as much of my hair as you can in five minutes.' Literally following these directions with zealous enthusiasm, the man quickly left his victim absolutely shorn to the skull, so that when Fawcett put on his hat it was far too large for him. A few minutes later he was shown into the drawing-room at the very minute of his appointment. He felt extremely embarrassed and sheepish coming in his despoiled condition, but his hostess, rising to meet him, exclaimed with as much tact as concealed surprise: 'O Mr. Fawcett, what an improvement! I have never before been able to see the beautiful shape of your head.' So the hostess tempered the wind to the shorn statesman. There was sufficient truth for art in her flattery, as Fawcett's head was really of an unusually fine shape, massive, rugged—even beautiful.

He loved to be read to.

He loved to be read to, and he kept a separate book for each friend who entertained him in this fashion. One day *The Rhyme of the Duchess May* was being read to him. In each stanza of the poem recurs the phrase 'Toll slowly.' The whole thing was admirably read—with pathetic emphasis on the refrain. One of the audience says: 'We all thought that Fawcett was asleep, but to our amusement, when the reader had finished, he said enthusiastically, with his generous voice, "Thank you very much; beautifully read, but don't you think that you might have left out that 'told slowly'?"

HENRY FAWCETT AND HIS FATHER

Salisbury Close.

He continued a frequent visitor at Salisbury, and always fitted in with the home ways. His parents had come to pass their closing year in a house in the Cathedral Close. Opposite the house there was a stretch of old wall, where before breakfast Fawcett used to walk quite by himself, enjoying a seclusion and peace such as was his in the court of his old Cambridge College. The gates of the close are shut at eleven o'clock every night. Miss Fawcett tells the following: 'As Henry liked to walk the last thing at night before going to bed, and as it was not always convenient for one of us to accompany him, we arranged for him to go with the gate closer on his rounds. So regularly, when Harry was at home, the gate closer's voice would be heard at half-past ten, "I've come for Mr. Harry," and together they would sally forth and lock the ancient gates about the close.' The scheme worked admirably to the entire satisfaction of Fawcett, and to the delight of the watchman, who, like the rest of the world, found Fawcett a stimulating and cheering companion. He awakened the seeing man's interest in the beauty of the cathedral which they passed in their nightly patrol, and often asked if a different planet had yet appeared on the horizon, if the moon could be seen over the church tower, or if the clouds were obscuring the stars.

The New Forest in peril.

Though he had passed his childhood on the edge of the New Forest, it is doubtful if Fawcett ever saw its beauties excepting with his mind's eye and by the help of his friends' description.

In the seventies he was fond of going there and combining the comfort and joy that he always found in his walk by the great trees with a fishing expedition at Ibbesley. Here he liked to stay with his fisher friend Tizard and his good wife, sharing their homely meals and chat; the place abounded in birds whose singing delighted him. It was here that he caught the huge salmon that graced the table at his father's and mother's golden wedding feast.

On these fishing expeditions he heard of the mania for money-making that threatened to rout the ancient spirit of romance which for centuries had lived in the seclusion of the great oaks and beeches. One enterprising surveyor said that the old wood should be cleared 'smack smooth.' The patrician ancient trees were being replaced by symmetrical lines of Scotch firs planted for sacrifice by fire or for building purposes. Fawcett in answer to inquiry was informed that the woods would not be cleared till the House of Commons had come to a division on the treatment of open spaces. Not content with this rather vague answer, he moved that 'no ornamental timber should be felled, and no timber whatever should be cut except for necessary purposes, whilst legislation was pending.' This resolution came none too soon and 'stood between the forest and the axe' for six years. The official point of view was that the term 'public' was misused; it really meant taxpayers, not tourists, nor even the neighbouring residents. The official duty consisted in making an income for the nation and making the most of the property of the Heir Apparent, so that he might make a better bargain on the next settlement of the Civil List. No resolution of the House of Commons could prevent the commissioner in charge of the New Forest from performing his duties, which were similar to those of a trustee of a settled estate.

The Forest—Health and Art.

Fawcett received signed petitions protesting against the devastation of the forest. In 1875 the Government, this time a Conservative Government, appointed a select committee on the condition of the New Forest. Fawcett gave evidence and spoke forcibly. 'The forest should be preserved as a national park. Any money which could be made by its enclosure was not worth considering in comparison with the effects upon the health, happiness, and morality of the people. Even arguing the matter from a purely economical point of view, the influence of the forest on the health and artistic faculties of the people had a far greater money value than that of the mere timber.' His comment of the effect of the beauty of the forest on the 'artistic faculties of the people' must have been peculiarly impressive; that a blind man could see so true, plead so wisely and far-seeingly for the best influence that his fellows could get from the right of those historic glades. Fawcett suggested that these honest, if penny-wise, stewards could ease their consciences by accepting the liberal compensation which the nation would be glad to pay. It was a mere superstition to feel that though neither the Crown nor the nation wished it, there was need to treat the forest as it would be treated by a timber merchant. He wisely pointed out that the Secretary of the Treasury had four years before used the same arguments to good purpose on behalf of the Thames Embankment Gardens. The committee speedily reported, and an Act was passed to preserve the ancient woods, and stop destructive enclosures, and the Verderer's Court was reconstituted, so as to represent the commoners more effectually.

Fawcett versus Ruskin.

It is when dwelling on this fight of Fawcett's for beauty versus money that it is amusing to realise that he was once challenged by Ruskin to a public debate — Fawcett to defend the political economy of his day against Ruskin's charge that it was radically opposed to Christianity. Fawcett wisely realised that they would have no common meeting-ground and refused to enter the lists.

'The monstrous Notion.'

The general questions of enclosures had still to be settled. The old method had been stopped for all time in Fawcett's Battle of Wisley Common, but no new machinery had been substituted. Bills were brought in two or three times, but failed to win sufficient support to be carried. In 1876 Lord Cross, the Home Secretary, brought in a Bill which showed a distinct advance in public opinion. Nevertheless, it did not satisfy the Commons Preservation Society. Next, the chairman of the society, Mr. Shaw Lefevre, now Lord Eversley, moved a resolution embodying the enactment of provisions and safeguards. The Bill was supported by a speaker who at the same time attacked what he chose to call 'the monstrous notion,' *i.e.* that the inhabitants of large towns had a right to wander over distant commons as they pleased. Fawcett, who also supported the Bill in a vigorous speech, swooped down, seized this 'monstrous notion' and held it aloft for admiration and support, and contended that the commons were a great and valuable possession for the people of the entire country.' He had again to insist that the bill did not adequately protect the labourers nor provide sufficient security against a ruthless enclosure of commons. He pointed out that 'under the old Enclosure Commission, 5,500,000 acres had been added to the estates of great proprietors, whilst villagers by the hundred had lost their rights of pasture, and now found it difficult to provide milk for their children. Yet the commission which had used this procedure was still to be trusted.' 'The worst and most mischievous of all economies,' he declared, 'was that which aggrandised a few, and made a paltry addition to the sum-total of wealth by shutting out the poor from fresh air and lovely scenery.' The bill passed through the committee, doggedly, though not very successfully, opposed by Fawcett and his friends.

Lord Eversley and Fawcett succeeded later in amending the procedure to be followed by the Enclosure Commissioners. The Commissioners were instructed that they must have proof that any proposed enclosure should be of real benefit to the neighbourhood as well as to private interests. Furthermore, every enclosure scheme had to be submitted to a standing committee of the House of Commons of which Fawcett was one of the first members.

Charm of Home.

The unfailing charm of Fawcett's home life was a constant delight and rest to him. Mrs. Fawcett's share in his career was of the greatest possible moment. Their only child Philippa began to be a source of great pleasure, and she enjoyed being with her father on his country expeditions as much as he delighted in having her with him.

Declaring firmly that he believed in at least eleven hours' skating, this serious statesman would often ponder deeply, as he thoughtfully rubbed his blue glasses and replaced them on his nose, how with ingenuity it would be possible to contrive to fit in another hour on the ice. He not only skated by himself, depending only on the voice of his companion to steer him, but he insisted that his wife, daughter, secretary, and two maids should all turn out to have a good time with him. Only the cook, on the uncontrovertible score of old age, was excused.

Little Philippa greatly enjoyed accompanying her father, and whistling in order to guide him. When she was about nine years old she had returned from a wonderful skate, when she had steered him in the customary fashion. She told her mother all about it and what fun they had had, on a particularly difficult route, her father depending solely on her piping to guide him. 'And what did you whistle?' asked the mother. 'Oh, just "Gentle Jesus,"' came the prompt reply.

Hymns.

Perhaps it is not amiss to indicate here the complete control that this small person exercised over her giant father. At this period of her life she had been imbued by her nurse with an intense devoutness. One Sunday morning he was singing to himself: it is only proper to say that the word singing is not an exact term, as all his friends and family are agreed that he was incapable of producing melody or sweet noises. His tiny daughter popped her head in at the crack of the door, saying solemnly: 'You mustn't sing, it's Sunday!' 'Are you sure?' asked Fawcett. 'Wait,' was the answer; closing the door his mentor disappeared, doubtless to consult with the nurse who had filled her with so much theological technique. Again the child appeared at the crack in the door, saying briefly: 'If it's hymns you may, if it isn't you mayn't,' and the singing ceased abruptly!

The sanctity of Open Spaces.

Open spaces, especially those near the big towns, had in the railway companies another and most powerful enemy. It was so much easier to take a railway across a common than through the neighbouring enclosed land, that there arose a serious risk that the commons though at last secured for the people, would still be despoiled of their freshness and beauty. Fawcett was quick to perceive this, and to try to save the open spaces from such invasions of their sanctity. He was characteristically amused once by the suggestion of some more prudent members of the Commons Preservation Society that he might weaken their position by failure. It was not by fear of defeat that he so often succeeded in turning defeat into victory. He never hesitated in his attack. Even when Postmaster-General he voted against his colleague, Mr. Chamberlain, the President of the Board of Trade, on a question of railway encroachment on Wimbledon Common.

It is a beautiful thing for all of us who have the privilege of enjoying the glory of the commons and forests of England to appreciate that that pleasure has been kept for us, and for countless others for all time, largely by the valiant fight and generous labours of a man who, though he loved them as he loved light, freedom and justice, and gave part of his life to save them, could only see them through the eyes of others.

Lord Morley takes Fawcett [on] a walk.

Lord Morley tells of Fawcett on these lands which he saved for the poor. Fawcett had been walking on Lord Morley's arm over the Wimbledon Commons, with that vigour and enjoyment in the exercise which he invariably found. They paused on a hill. Lord Morley, impressed with the unusual loveliness of the sunset and its ineffable melancholy, was startled to hear Fawcett beside him ask wistfully: 'Morley, is the sunset very beautiful?' 'Yes,' was the answer. 'Ah, I thought so,' came the comment before a long silence, in which the blind man seemed to be taking in the exquisite scene spread before his unseeing eyes.

We know how Fawcett's deep love of nature and beauty was a strong factor of his very being. He loved the forest and the hills, the fields and the skies, and above all the rivers.

Following the Boat Race.

Until nearly the end of his life, Fawcett rarely missed the Oxford and Cambridge rowing contests. It was a matter of course to see him 'looking over' the crew of the college 'eight' and expressing his opinion frankly about its fitness, or eagerly 'watching' a race. He followed the University boat race on one occasion in a launch, and in the keenest excitement continually asked his friend, 'How are they going now, Morgan? How near are they now?'

The race gained much zest for Fawcett from the motion of the tug from which he watched it, from the noise of the water lapping against the side of the boat, the splash of the oars, the occasional spray dashed in his face as the little ship darted to hasten its course by benefiting in an opening in the crowd of craft. The cheers of the spectators, the calling of the coxswains to the straining crews, and even the occasional tooting of an unmannerly tug, all gave colour to the picture for the blind man. The river's fascination perhaps even increased for him after he could not see it.

Safeguarding the Rivers.

When the Thames needed a protector to safeguard its loveliness, it was the blind man who eagerly urged that an organisation, similar to the Commons Preservation Society, should be formed to protect the river, and it was through his advice that a Select Committee with this object was later appointed. He also took occasion to support Lord Bryce in his efforts to abolish the system which hampered the public in their enjoyment of the beauties of the Scottish Highlands.

Stephen speaks of his readiness to refuse prominence if he thought that others could serve better than he, of his eagerness 'to meet the strength of the opposite case,' to see his opponent's point of view and to judge it generously; he dwells on the great interest he took in private life in considering impartially and thoughtfully his friends' problems, so that his advice to them was of unusual value. The whole chapter of this fight for the rights of those who were least able to fight for themselves, sustained and led by a man who could not see or enjoy, saving vicariously, what he was fighting for, is as heroic as any in history. He faced the danger of losing his hard-won position, and often alone made the decision to act against the advice of his friends and his own interests and to stand for the right. In his simple direct plea for justice he never rested until he got what was the people's due, and what must remain for all time a living monument to his singleness of purpose and chivalrous bravery.

THE MEMBER FOR INDIA

'Let thy dauntless mind
Still ride in triumph over all mischance.'

SHAKESPEARE.

'Not from without us only, from
Within can come upon us light.'

CHAPTER XXII

WHAT INDIA PAID

India pays for English Hospitality—Royal English generosity to India paid for by India—How to deal with an angry opponent—Indian Finance and the poor Ryot—Gratitude from India—How Fawcett prepared his Speeches.

The Sultan's Ball.

The purpose of this chapter is not to comment on the condition of India, and of its government in Fawcett's time, but through these new labours of his to know him better, to show how gallantly he fought for a poor remote people, and how poignantly he brought their needs before their English fellow-subjects. It was a work he was peculiarly fitted to do. His vigorous action, his picturesque personality, his gift for singling out a weak point, perhaps trifling in itself, and making it a vivid symbol of wrong policy, all helped Englishmen unfamiliar with India to realise better their responsibilities to a country in whose destinies they were so closely concerned.

Fawcett once said that in his undergraduate days he had picked up a book on India which attracted him to the subject. His comments in his schoolboy essays have been noted. It is possible that Mill and other friends of his closely connected with India stimulated his interest. He referred to the country a good deal in his *Manual of Political Economy.*

He first dealt with Indian affairs publicly in 1867, and in most characteristic fashion. The Sultan of Turkey was about to visit England, and it was proposed to give a ball in his honour at the India Office. Fawcett demanded who was to foot the bill. He was told that India was to pay for this courtesy offered to the Sultan by the British, because the Sultan had been courteous in the matter of telegraphic communication between India and Europe.

India pays for English Hospitality.

Though Mill urged Fawcett not to protest, as there were greater abuses to be found, Fawcett could not quiet his resentment at this unfair distribution of the burden. Had not England benefited equally by the telegraphic communication, and should it not at least pay equally? So, when a motion was made for the list of invitations, with the usual Parliamentary pleasantries about the unfair selection of guests, Fawcett rose with true reluctance to strike a discordant note. He urged that the really important question was to determine by what justice the Secretary for India could tax the people of India for this entertainment. It might be proper for the officials themselves to give the entertainment. But why should the toiling peasant pay for it? At that very time there was famine in India, and the Indian press complained of the slowness of relief measures. It would have new occasion for sarcasm, when a part of the much-needed Indian revenue was voted for an entertainment of smart folk in London.

His protest against this 'masterpiece of meanness,' as he afterwards called it, had little effect for the time being. But it aroused the attention of many in India, and began to make known to them the man whom they learned to call almost affectionately the 'Member for India.'

An Insolent Meddler.

When presenting a petition to the House of Commons from European residents and natives of India, who complained of the expenditure on public works and asked for greater economy, Fawcett moved that a commission be sent to India to obtain evidence on the spot—a motion that he afterwards withdrew. During the debate arising out of his motion, he was attacked with such asperity and lack of civility by one of the Under Secretaries of State, that it aroused the protest of other members. Fawcett was content to reply with a very characteristic maxim. 'Five years' experience in the House,' he said, 'had taught him that a member was always right in bringing forward a question, when the fact of his bringing it forward caused the minister concerned to lose his temper.' On another occasion the same antagonist warned Fawcett that his love of competition was becoming a fetish. But Fawcett smilingly retaliated, 'Beware of the fetish of officialism.' Good advice for many!

Fawcett's stand from the first was taken so surely and firmly, that his ground could not be cut from under him. His success was merely a question of work and time. Part of his power lay in his frank realisation of his own limitations.

Supporting a family on fourpence halfpenny a day.

He had no special knowledge of Indian religion and customs, and was not competent to judge questions of internal policy. But the financial relations between England and India, as well as the methods of dealing with finance in India itself, were well within the compass of his clear mind. With these he proposed to deal exhaustively. He knew whether the balance-sheets shown by Indian statesmen were intelligible or not, whether charges made to India were just, and he set himself with a will to study these questions. And to them he knew how to give a most intimately personal touch. He was an untravelled man, and lived within the isolation of his blindness. But he had the great gift of realising habitually the existence of the world beyond his experience. He made England understand that India is no rich country from the Arabian Nights, but a poor country, where the ryot, the peasant of India, had but fourpence halfpenny a day to keep himself and his family, where taxes were increased only with great hardship to the poor, and where of all places money must not be wasted.

In 1870, in a long and technical speech, he criticised the Indian Budget. He complained that it was brought on so late in the session that there was no time for proper discussion, and urged that a committee on Indian finance should be appointed. In this speech, which showed his careful study of the whole Budget, he singled out one item for especial scorn. The Queen's second son, the Duke of Edinburgh, had recently journeyed through India, and had distributed royal gifts amounting in value to £10,000. These had been paid for out of the Indian revenues, that is to say, by the Indian taxpayers themselves!

The Prime Minister agreed that the Indian Budget should be presented earlier in the session, and the next year adopted Fawcett's proposal to appoint a committee on Indian finance. It sat for four years, and Fawcett was a hard-working member of it, and a most effective one.

The committee, urged by Fawcett, asked for native witnesses, and two Hindoos were sent to England to give evidence, and their expenses were paid by the Government.

Mr. Nadabhai Naoroji, one of them, said that he wrote a letter telling of the evidence which he had to give, and then appeared before the Finance Committee. The chairman was not sympathetic, and made things as uncomfortable as possible for him. But when Fawcett, with whom Naoroji had discussed matters previously, undertook the examination, by a series of apt questions he brought out all the distinguished Hindoo had to say. Mr. Naoroji adds: 'This was an instance of the justice and fearlessness with which he wanted to treat this country. As I saw him pleading our cause, I felt awe and veneration as for a superior being.'

Grateful messages from India.

In Miss Maria Fawcett's dining-room there hangs at this day a long hand-written document, with a beautifully illuminated gold and coloured border. It was sent to her brother from a remote city in India in 1873, to thank him for the work he had done. Too long to quote in full, a sentence from it may show how Fawcett was regarded in India. 'We view with feelings of inexpressible delight your efforts to enlighten your countrymen of the wants and grievances of the millions of Her Majesty's subjects living in a country so far from the seat of government, and our feeling of admiration is heightened into that of reverence on learning that you are labouring in this cause of philanthropy under great disadvantages, among which the great physical disability which Providence has pleased to impose upon you is much to be regretted.'

Distinguished now as an able critic on Indian finance, Fawcett had an extensive correspondence with residents of India, and with members of the Indian Civil Service, and neglected no opportunity to increase his knowledge of Indian affairs.

Appreciative resolutions were sent to him from many native Indian associations. At a meeting in Calcutta an address was voted to him and also one to 'the Mayor of Brighton thanking the constituency for returning such a worthy representative and disinterested friend of India.' He was frequently begged to present petitions stating the grievances of the native and non-official community.

He helped privately, as well as publicly, as many a poor Indian student or petitioner came to know. When, however, Fawcett was urged to represent the grievances of certain Indian rulers, he refused, saying quaintly that 'he was too poor a man to have anything to do with princes.'

An Optimist.

Mr. Justice Scott said, speaking of the ideal for which Fawcett worked: 'It is not enough for us Englishmen to say that we have given to India order, peace, security and justice, roads, railroads, and other material benefits of Western civilisation, but it should be our duty to ourselves and in co-operation with the people of India in the great task of education, private, social and political, never to rest content till every individual of the teeming masses of India can take an intelligent part as a citizen in the management of their own concerns. This is a great idea. It may seem the Utopian dream of an optimist. Mr. Fawcett was no doubt an optimist.'

Fawcett most powerfully influenced people by his speeches. His appearance was arresting and interesting, while his brave disregard of his blindness claimed instant sympathy and admiration. His voice, which was unusually powerful, softened in tone with years, and his language grew less severe; he uttered each word clearly, and what he said was clearly thought out. What he wanted was never for himself. What he fought for was invariably to help some one less fortunate, less free, less happy, than the blind man who pleaded so earnestly.

He delivered two speeches in 1872 and 1873 on the Indian Budgets of those years which an adversary said 'he considered to be the most remarkable intellectual efforts he had ever heard.' Of course Fawcett, unlike other speakers, had no notes to help him, yet he gave an exposition of complex questions with a clearness which might have raised the envy of the most accomplished Chancellor of the Exchequer.

How Fawcett prepared his Speeches.

The way he prepared his speeches is interesting. First, he would master the vital facts and figures he wanted. Then he would press into his service some friend well up on the subject with which he wished to deal, and together they would go over the ground until Fawcett felt that the facts were arranged so as to express most clearly and pithily his contention.

Lucid arrangement helped his memory. His object was primarily to be clear, to say a thing as well as he could. He did not hesitate to repeat the same illustrations and statements, and paid little attention to rhetoric, epigram or elegance. He wished to hammer certain leading principles into people's heads, and he did this so effectively that they stuck there, and he pressed his points so vividly and insistently that he made his audiences, no matter where he found them, usually become his supporters, and even workers for his policy.

Photo. Mansell

HENRY FAWCETT

From a painting by Sir Hubert von Herkomer

On one occasion Fawcett spoke on India for nearly two hours. He had the House absolutely in his hand the whole of that time, and never once had to hark back. The figures that he dealt with were exceedingly complicated and numerous. Later an M.P. congratulated him and expressed his surprise at his wonderful memory. Fawcett, with his habitual modesty, said, 'There is nothing strange about it. You know I see the thing mentally as I suppose you see whatever you are looking upon now; really that is the difference.' The M.P. replied, 'Yes, but it doesn't account for it at all. I see and forget—you see and don't forget, there's the difference.'

Sympathy from Suffering.

A Cambridge professor said of Fawcett when he began to make those remarkable speeches on Indian affairs: 'We, I think, were mainly struck with the extraordinary intellectual feats that they were for a man under his calamity; but the effect produced in India was of a different and profounder kind. There was the sense of the largeness of heart of the statesman who had known suffering, and a gratitude for his broad sympathy with all whom he could protect against what he conceived to be oppression of any kind.'

No time in Parliament for India.

He did not hesitate to speak on Indian affairs to his constituency, and to ask of them their sympathy and interest. At a meeting in Brighton he said that the most trumpery question ever brought before Parliament, a wrangle over the purchase of a picture or a road through a park excited more interest than the welfare of the many millions of our Indian fellow-subjects. Constituencies were said to take no interest in the subject. They would be some day forced to take an interest, if affairs were neglected in the future as they had been in the past. 'The people of India have not votes; they cannot bring so much pressure to bear upon Parliament as can be brought by one of our great railway companies; but with some confidence I believe that I shall not be misinterpreting your wishes if, as your representative, I do whatever can be done by one humble individual to render justice to the defenceless and powerless.'

That last sentence could be taken as his policy and motto through life. Could there be a more valiant one for a blind man, or for any one fighting against great odds for the right? 'I do whatever can be done by one humble individual to render justice to the defenceless and powerless.' He does not limit whom or where. There are no limitations. That they are defenceless and powerless is all the recommendation which they need to claim his warmest interest and ceaseless effort to help them to find the way out of their misery.

CHAPTER XXIII

THE 'ONE MAN WHO CARED FOR INDIA'

Defeated at Brighton—Spectacles and the Man—Elected for Hackney.

Effect of Speeches in India.

In spite of many warnings that his Indian policy would be unpopular, his adherence to his high ideal of a truly Imperial citizenship proved a good campaign asset, and Fawcett's constituents were proud of him, and absorbed in his expositions of Indian affairs.

Notwithstanding that he lost his seat at Brighton at the next general election, he was soon in the House again, representing another constituency. The prominence of his position in the House of Commons and out of it was much enhanced by the power of his Indian speeches.

His popularity in Cambridge was unquestioned. On his return to residence there, his home was a merry meeting-place for his many friends old and new. His original ways were a byword. He once began a new acquaintanceship in this fashion. Shaking hands warmly with a young student who had just been introduced, Fawcett said jovially, 'What do you do—ride, or row or fish? I smoke!'

In speaking of Fawcett, the present head Master of Trinity used these words: 'We all had a veneration for Fawcett, and loved to see the way he won every one. A friend of all of ours with whom Fawcett stayed tried us very much by insisting that all his guests should go to bed by ten o'clock. One of them vowed that "he'd be hanged if he would go to bed at ten o'clock." We were greatly relieved and amused that when Fawcett appeared on the scene, his conversation so completely charmed his host that it was impossible to get him to bed until long after midnight.'

Mastership of Trinity Hall.

When a vacancy occurred in the Mastership of Trinity Hall, Fawcett was asked to stand, and though he retired from the candidature in favour of Sir Henry Maine, it is an interesting evidence of Fawcett's close interest in his old college that no new interests could weaken.

At this time his chief exercise seems to have been riding. A friend who often accompanied him gives this description of one adventurous morning ride: 'His riding was like the driving of Jehu. He was entirely fearless, seemed to know all the road, the turnings, the signposts, and the houses, where the turf began that was good to go on, and where the horse must be allowed to walk.

Spectacles and the Man.

'We were going together at a moderate pace on his favourite road. I was a yard in front; suddenly I heard a noise as of a fall, and looking back saw to my horror Fawcett lying on the ground, and his horse standing quietly by. How it happened I don't know. I jumped down in terror, but was soon reassured by Fawcett calling out in his natural voice, "Just look for my spectacles, will you?" When I had helped him up and brought him to his horse, he remounted without the least appearance of flurry or alarm. He explained to me as we cantered on, that he thought that in case of a fall, he was in less danger than a seeing man, as he did not attempt to move or struggle. He seemed to think no more of his fall, beyond expressing a wish that I should not speak of it at home, and thus cause alarm and nervousness when he was riding again.'

Enjoying the Sunset.

This courage is the more remarkable in view of the fact that Fawcett once said: 'The happiest moments I spend in my life are when I am in the companionship of some friend who will forget that I have lost my eyesight, who will talk to me as if I could see, who will describe to me the persons I meet, a beautiful sunset, or scenes of great beauty through which we may be passing. For so wonderful is the adaptability of the human mind, that when for instance some scene of great beauty has been described to me, I recall that scene in after years, and I speak about it in such a manner that sometimes I have to check myself and consider for a moment whether the impression was produced when I had my sight or was conveyed by the description of another.'

It is not conceivable that the man who so thoroughly saw through the vision given to him by others, could have been deficient in the power to imagine vividly, acutely, all possible dangers. It meant a very deliberate courage to overcome all slowness and hesitancy — to gallop alone, trusting entirely to his horse to save him from, may be, serious collisions. Yet, so complete was Fawcett's self-mastery that he thrust fear utterly behind him, and found only hearty, high-spirited joy in his outings.

Hackney. A model campaign.

This same courage stood him in good stead in the general election in 1874, which resulted in a great victory for the Conservatives. In Brighton both the Liberal candidates were thrown out, though Fawcett polled forty-nine more votes than before. Within six weeks he was again an M.P., this time enthusiastically elected for Hackney; and the management of his election for that borough was so inexpensive that it was long cited as a model of electioneering efficiency and economy.

The Indian papers spoke strongly of his 'unique position,' and a fund of £400 was raised and transmitted to England to pay the expenses of another contest. It arrived too late, but went towards the expenses of the contest at Hackney in 1880.

Another sum of £350 was then raised in India, which was placed in the hands of trustees with a view to a future election, and in due time was devoted to some purpose connected with India.

Fawcett's first speech to his Hackney constituents was delivered in March. What he said there, then and later, was distinguished by his fearless and frank adherence to what were considered unpopular principles. He denounced what he deemed the unworthy competition between Gladstone and Disraeli, saying that when the former announced that in case of his election he would repeal the Income Tax, the latter promptly announced that he would do the same. Fawcett considered that neither could carry out this promise, and that it was merely a discreditable bid for votes. He said that he would continue in his efforts for India, then threatened anew by famine.

The Times.

The *Saturday Review*, not usually favourable to his party, hoped for his return as the 'one man,' out of official circles, who cared for India. The *Times* said 'he offended publicans by refusing to use their houses as committee rooms; he offended the advocates of the Permissive Bill by declaring his resolution to vote against it; he offended shopkeepers by his zeal in favour of the co-operative movement; he offended working men by his opposition to the latest movement for limiting the hours of labour of adult women; he offended old-fashioned Liberals, and Liberals who are getting old-fashioned, by his persistent advocacy of reforms that had not come within the range of their education when they were young; and Liberals of a later growth remembered how often Fawcett had found himself unable to acquiesce in Mr. Gladstone's policy and plans. Yet he must have secured the support of men of all these sections, who concurred in sending him to Parliament, because they believed that his presence there would be advantageous, in spite of errors of opinion which each section in turn lamented.'

His short absence between his defeat at Brighton and his fresh appearance as the representative for Hackney was sincerely regretted in the House of Commons on all sides. Warm friends missed his genial personality and the jovial meetings at his seat, whence many merry stories and much gossip emanated. Those who saw Fawcett casually found it difficult to believe that he was blind. It was his unfailing habit to turn to the person to whom he was speaking as if he saw them. He knew his way about the House of Commons so well that he was quick and sure in all his movements. He would cross the floor of the House and, bowing to the Speaker, take his seat with familiar assurance. His father used often to come up from Salisbury, and Fawcett would take him to the privileged strangers' seats under the gallery, and bring his Parliamentary friends to talk to the old gentleman.

One of the favourite ways of drawing attention to departmental misdeeds is to ask questions of the Minister of State concerned to be answered by him at the beginning of the sitting. These questions were sent up in writing and then read aloud to the House by the members who asked them. The Rt. Hon. Thomas Burt, one of the first working-class representatives, and an old friend of Fawcett's, says: 'Mr. Fawcett often put long questions, and he repeated them word for word as they were printed on the order paper, never a slip, never the slightest hesitation.'

The hard-worked Hen.

Fawcett was at once added to the committee on Indian finance appointed a few days before his election. This was the fourth year that this committee had worked. *Punch* said that it reminded him 'of the hen that laid so many eggs she could never come to the hatching of any.' And indeed it never published a report, though it collected a great deal of most valuable evidence.

It was before this committee that Lord Salisbury gave evidence on the difficulty for an Indian Secretary of State to withstand the demands of the Treasury. Continued resistance on his part was 'to stop the machine.' 'so,' said Fawcett, 'you must either stop the machine, or resign, or go on tacitly submitting to injustice.' 'I should accept the statement,' replied Lord Salisbury, 'barring the word tacitly. I should go on submitting with loud remonstrances.'

But a strong echo in the public conscience would be necessary for these remonstrances to be of any value to India, and this is what Fawcett saw.

CHAPTER XXIV

FAMINE, TURKS AND INDIANS

Punch and Fawcett—The Indian Famine—Parliamentary Interest
aroused in India—Bulgarian Atrocities—Afghanistan War—
Gladstone's Faith in Fawcett—A £9,000,000 Mistake.

He was becoming one of the most prominent figures in the House of Commons, and as such is frequently mentioned in the political diary with which *Punch* has amused more than two generations. *Punch* gives vivid glimpses of our hero 'hitting out in fine style,' giving 'a well deserved rap over the knuckles' to some not too scrupulous speaker. Then he is 'the blind gentleman who cannot see things in his way like other people, and so will not be turned aside'; or 'One of the biggest wigs on India.' On a night of great debate 'First in the lists was that ablest of intractables, Professor Fawcett, who not seeing when he bores others can defy the penalties of boredom in the strength of an honest purpose.' Finally, when energy was required 'Professor Fawcett danced over it.'

Then back to the quiet home across the river, and a peaceful time by his own fireside. In damp weather the tolling of Big Ben would ring clear over the water. Fawcett did not need to be told it was raining or to depend on the patter on the window panes for his knowledge. He knew it by the distinctive noises of the wet wheels of traffic. All the various noises of the London streets were acutely present to him: the uneven, slow hammer of a lame horse's hoofs, the short quick step of a donkey, and the whir of the two wheels of a coster's donkey-cart piled high with vegetables for Covent Garden, or the more rhythmic trot of a pair of carriage horses and the almost noiseless revolutions of the wheels of prosperous vehicles. He knew of fog by the muffled cries of the cabbies and the linkmen, or by the bewildering tooting of the river craft on the Thames.

In 1875 Gladstone retired from the Liberal leadership, and Lord Hartington was elected in his stead. The Liberals were a disorganised and despondent party, sitting in the coldest of cold shades of opposition. But there was nothing dispirited about Fawcett. In this session he reiterated two former war-cries: the one to reduce the expenses of Parliamentary candidates—a proposal which still had little support from either side of the House; the other, to insist with this Government as he had insisted with the former one, to bring on the debate on the Indian Budget in sufficient time for proper discussion. In the same session funds were voted to meet the expenses of the tour about to be made by the Prince of Wales in India. Fawcett was wishful that the whole cost of this voyage of good will should be met by England. But both Disraeli and Gladstone opposed him, and he was unable to get his point carried.

The Liberty of the Individual.

His strong belief in individual liberty gave Fawcett scant sympathy with that school of thought which was for controlling people into better conditions of living. When the Conservative Government brought in a bill for municipal action in cases of bad housing, and the premier happily misquoted 'sanitas sanitatum, omnia sanitas,' Fawcett was scornful. He considered it class legislation and paternally patronising in a way that few would understand to-day. He had the same feeling about the Factory Acts, except when they were to protect the most helpless. On the other hand, he was eager to extend the compulsory attendance of children at school, and urged it several times during this Parliament.

Empress of India.

Queen Victoria was proclaimed Empress of India at Delhi in 1877 amidst much stately ceremonial and much thundering of cannon.

Famine.

But the reverberations from the Imperial salute had hardly died away before ominous news was muttered of famine in Bengal. It proved only too true, and was very terrible in its effects. More than two million people died. Many endeavours were made to cope with the disaster, and also to provide better against its recurrence, in all of which Fawcett took deep interest. A month or two later it was proposed to remit the duty on cotton. Fawcett, although a strong free trader, opposed this, as he thought the change at this time would deal hardly with India.

In 1879 Fawcett published an article in the *Nineteenth Century*, called 'The New Departure in Finance,' in which he shows the changes that have been wrought. He points out, amongst other things, that in that year the Indian Budget was discussed in May instead of in August, and that it excited sufficient interest for the debate to last three nights, whereas in former years it was generally hurried over in the closing hours of the session. The vital importance of limiting taxation and reducing expenditure had been acknowledged by the highest authorities, and an obstacle had thus been surmounted which had hitherto stood in the way of all serious reforms. He insisted on the importance of developing the resources of the country, but objected to reckless borrowing for that purpose. He considered that the expenses could be reduced until there should be a fair surplus to spend on works of real value. He emphasised most particularly a policy always much in his mind. There might be a great saving of money, and a great gain politically, if more opportunity were given to the native races to be employed in Government posts. After calling attention to the heavy military expenditure, he ends with the expression of a hope that a new financial era is really being inaugurated.

Fawcett was surprised and amused at the way in which his essay was received with unanimous approval, and said that it showed 'the uncertainty of any forecast of the effect of an appeal to the public.' After years of labour apparently productive of little result, he had suddenly become an exponent of accepted principles.

He is now the great man. And a great man's jokes, however feeble, make their impress. But through this atmosphere we see the cheerful Fawcett of our ken, gay, brusque, and light-hearted.

He walks with a friend from Newmarket to Cambridge. The friend relates:

Fawcett and the Yokels.

'We stopped at a roadside inn for lunch; the country yokels stared, as well they might, at this strong-faced blind man, full of interest for the things they knew about. He insisted on paying more than the landlady asked, because he had taken all the crust off the loaf!

'I saw some one on the road whom I thought Fawcett ought to know, who passed with no sign of recognition. On inquiry from him why I thought he would know this man, I described him as some old fogey who looked like a member of the University. Later on I had occasion to talk to him about the strenuous exercise he often took, and hazarded a conjecture that he was as strong as any member of the House of Commons. His version, shouted out to his wife directly he got inside of his house, was that I had been calling him an old fogey, and had been trying to make up for it by calling him the strongest member of the House.'

'In the evening his wife or any friend present read aloud to him. I remember one evening, after I had been reading the *Spectator* to him, Mrs. Fawcett took up Trevelyan's *Life of Fox*, and read to him for some minutes; she then looked up and said, 'Harry, you are asleep!' He indignantly denied it, and to show that he had not been asleep said, "I have heard every word you said. I think we will have some of Fox's Life now." When informed that we had been reading it for ten minutes, he said, without being at all disconcerted, "Oh, have you, then go on!"'

The terrible Turks.

The Beaconsfield Government (for Disraeli was now Earl of Beaconsfield), which had begun its course so prosperously, had from 1876 onwards to meet difficulties arising from war in Eastern Europe. The Turks put down a rising in Bulgaria with inconceivable barbarity, and Beaconsfield's handling of the question gave great offence to many Englishmen. The sufferings of the Christians brought Gladstone out of his retirement and, in the first days of September, he published a pamphlet that was sold daily in its thousands. Within a fortnight Fawcett presided at a great meeting in Exeter Hall, the birthplace of so many crusades.

It is popularly supposed that it is particularly difficult for the blind to keep order or to compel attention. This idea has often been used as an objection to the blind as teachers or lecturers. As many things are true in the same degree of the blind person as of the seeing person. The practical question which should be asked in such cases is irrespective of blindness, and is: 'Has the man sufficient personality to be interesting and to command attention and respect?' Fawcett had. Both his blindness and his disregard of it compelled admiration, even reverence, while they added interest to what he said, and brought out the latent chivalrous, gracious qualities of his audience. It was probably far easier for him to preside at a meeting than it would have been for a sighted person of average calibre. He was not forced to keep order by himself, for most of the men at the meeting unconsciously helped the blind chairman by their sympathy and attention. Fawcett's natural quickness, keyed to high pitch by his blindness, made him swift to detect the slightest movement or half-murmured objection, and to catch the change of mood in the tones of a speaker who was, even unknown to himself, being turned from his original point.

No breach of procedure escaped this chairman, whose unseeing eyes seemed to watch the expression of each debater. To see Fawcett in the chair, dominating the other strong men with whom he worked, was a sight not to be forgotten. Rising to his great height, and looking around with his genial smile, he would open the meeting with a few words. If their quiet authority left no doubt but that there would be order, there was a pleasant marginal sense that it would be order not necessarily dreary or even unmixed with fun.

A striking proof of his popularity occurred at the National Conference in the following December. Gladstone was chief orator, but Fawcett, who was on the platform, was called for from the audience to add his words as well.

But the first popular indignation became overcast by a jealousy of Russian action, and when the House met its mood was hesitating and uncertain. But not Fawcett. In March he moved independently a resolution demanding that the European Powers should insist on adequate reforms, and led an attack on the Government, that claimed to have a spirited foreign policy which was really a do-nothing policy. The Conservatives cried, horror-stricken, that Fawcett wanted a 'bloody war.' The Liberal front bench said that the resolution was inopportune, and they suggested it should be withdrawn. To this Fawcett felt obliged to consent, as a weak following from his own party would have made a most discouraging vote.

Two months later Gladstone brought in a resolution on the subject, but thought it unwise to go further than he could persuade the front bench to follow him. How eagerly he urged the Liberal leaders, and how reluctantly they consented, was not known at the time, and the weakness of Gladstone's resolution was a great disappointment to Fawcett. He spoke vigorously at this May debate, and *Punch* says of 'this blind, brave Mr. Fawcett,' 'And it do me good to hear one so downright in these over timid times. And do call a spade a spade as plain as ever I hear.... And Mr. Gladstone did speak mighty well to the same time as Mr. Fawcett, only sharper and stronger and brisker and fiercer all at once as is his wont.'

Fawcett, who had so lately been treated as a firebrand, found himself on the other side of the scales when in the next year's phase of the question Beaconsfield's Government became bellicose, and moved troops from India to the Mediterranean. Beaconsfield sided more and more strongly with the Turks as the question wrapped itself up into those complications whose orchestration is called the Concert of Europe. It was generally felt that these troops were on hand to help the Turks.

The Bengal Tiger.

Their removal from India to Malta roused Fawcett on two issues—the possibility of helping the Turks and the making of unfair demands on India. He again attacked the Ministers, or as *Punch* says, 'had it out with the Government about bringing the Bengal Tiger into European Waters.'

The Eastern question was to continue to disturb Europe, creating suspicions and fostering disagreements. Its first dramatic fruit was at the other end of the Russian dominions, where Afghanistan lies between the threatening borders of the Russian and British Empires. The Amir of Afghanistan, 'an earthen pipkin between two iron pots,' was wooed by England and by Russia, but desired the attentions of neither. But to prove his neutrality was impossible. The Indian Government accused him of favouring Russia, and a clumsy diplomacy led finally to war.

Fawcett denounced at Bethnal Green, and again at Hackney, the underhand conduct of the Indian Government towards the Amir, and demanded that Parliament should be summoned. He argued from the opinions of high authorities that an occupation of the capital city, Cabul, would involve an intolerable burden upon Indian finances.

To shield the Indian Taxpayer.

When Parliament met to approve the expenditure incurred in Afghanistan, Fawcett, seconded by Mr. Gladstone, proposed that the cost of the war should not be thrown upon India. Once more he was defending the Indian tax-payer. He complained that when it was a question of declaring war, the Government had boasted that they were carrying out a great Imperial policy; when it was a question of paying for the war, they represented it as a mere border squabble. The course adopted by Government was unpopular, because it was marked by meanness and 'entire absence of generosity.' He declared that his constituents at Hackney would prefer to pay their fair share of the expense. His motion was rejected by 235 to 125. Fawcett returned to the charge in the next session, when a financial arrangement was proposed for apportioning the burden between England and India. Fawcett, in criticising, showed that India would have to pay twice as much as England. He was again seconded by Gladstone, but was again unsuccessful.

Gladstone's Faith in Fawcett's knowledge.

A story told of Fawcett at this time shows how real was the respect for his knowledge and exactness. He was staying at a week-end house-party in the country. Gladstone was there, and said to him, 'What do you think of the news of Afghanistan? I have not read the papers and I have a speech to make on the subject. I have been at the Corpus Christi library, looking at the Parker manuscripts, comparing the 39 Articles, so that I have had no time.' Fawcett told him about the Afghanistan conditions so fully and accurately that Gladstone, without having any further information, made a long and most telling speech about them in Parliament.

The importance to Gladstone of the Parker manuscript as compared with the Afghanistan complications is highly characteristic; we can imagine Fawcett's amusement that Gladstone should become absorbed in an academic question of theological punctilio, for such it would seem to him, when there was such really vital matters at issue.

Before Parliament met again, Fawcett had accepted his appointment as Post-master-General on condition that he would be free 'to take part in Indian debates.' But the great demands made on his time left little energy for other matters.

A Mistake of Nine Million Pounds, no one to blame.

He expressed himself in 1880 at length on the Indian Budget, when an error of nine millions in the accounts of the Afghan War came before the House. He showed how it emphasised the need of the precautions which he had urged on the Finance Committee, especially when it appeared that no one could be held responsible for this great carelessness. It was a comfort for him to be able to approve, in the main, the trend which the Indian policy continued to take, and that what he had laboured for so devotedly became the policy of the Government.

In reviewing his struggles for India, several things about him stand out force-fully. The fearlessness with which he took up a dangerous position, and by his very bravery made it safe ground. The scornful way he pushed aside whatever he considered spurious or unworthy. He gained not only the love of those whose battles he fought, but also the respect and goodwill of his adversaries.

Sir William Lee Warner says, 'His great fear was that India might be saddled with charges which the British Treasury ought to bear; and the poverty of the ryot afflicted him as if he suffered himself.' This suffering for others, so characteristic of Fawcett, was another common trait which he had with Lincoln, who we remember said that 'he didn't pull the wretched pig out of the mire for the pig's sake, but to take the pain out of his own heart.'

In recognition of her husband's great service, a beautiful necklace was sent in gratitude from India for Mrs. Fawcett, and a sumptuous tea-service was sent to him, which was inscribed, 'Presented to the Rt. Honble. Henry Fawcett, M.P., by his native friends and admirers in Bombay, India, June 1880.'

With no aid save his great heart and tremendous energy, he had won his battle for India. Despite his galvanic talk and pioneering energy, he had shown great diplomacy. His stand had been made on the rock bed of honesty, and he had given no quarter to deceit or self-seekers. In serving his country as he would serve himself he had found his path of happiness.

A NEW KIND OF POSTMASTER-GENERAL

'You can force your heart and nerve and sinew to serve your turn long after they have gone—and so hold on when there is nothing in you except the will which says hold on.'

—KIPLING.

CHAPTER XXV

LIBERALS IN POWER

General Expectation that Fawcett would join the Cabinet—The Importance of a Fish—Postmaster-General—Queen Victoria interested—Post Office Problems—Scientific Business Management anticipated—Women's Work—A Likeness to Lincoln.

His Preparation.

It is doubtful if anything but incessant struggles, the single-handed upholding of forlorn hopes, the fighting of battles with no other ammunition than irrefutable fact, and finally, the frequent victory over overwhelming difficulties, could have fitted Fawcett for the great task which lay before him. No easier life could have given him the instinctive grip of the essential, the sympathy which reads men truly, and the eagerness to serve the least of them which fitted this blind man to take efficient command of an army of over 90,000 people, to inspire them with an *esprit de corps* which they had heretofore lacked, and incidentally to fill them with a sense of gratitude, loyalty and affection to their chief. This is what Fawcett did with the Post Office department of England.

The General Election of 1880 returned the Liberals into power, with Gladstone once more at their head. Fawcett's prominence before the public had grown so steadily and surely, and his attack on the last Government had been so strong, that he was widely accepted as a probable member of the new Government.

The Importance of a Fish.

He ran down to Cambridge just before he received his appointment. All who knew him there were on the *qui vive*, eagerly awaiting the good tidings which they expected any minute. A friend called, in the hope of gathering news. Fawcett greeted him cordially, and went on to ask, 'Have you seen that fish I caught yesterday?' Characteristic this, to discuss fish, not politics, at the crisis of his career.

Mr. Gladstone offered the Postmaster-Generalship to Fawcett in April 1880. The following letter was written to his parents the day after:

'MY DEAR FATHER AND MOTHER,—You will I know all be delighted to hear that last night I received a most kind letter from Gladstone offering me the Postmaster-Generalship. It is the office which Lord Hartington held when Gladstone was last in power.

I shall be a Privy Councillor, but shall not have a seat in the Cabinet. I believe there was some difficulty raised about my having to confide Cabinet secrets; apparently because of the dependence on others for handling correspondence.

Queen Victoria interested.

This objection, I think, time will remove. I did not telegraph to you the appointment at first because Gladstone did not wish it to be known until it was formally confirmed by the Queen; but he told me in my interview with him this morning that he was quite sure that the Queen took a kindly interest in my appointment.'

He adds that Mr. Gladstone said 'that he has given me the appointment in order that I might have time to speak in Indian and other debates.' He goes on to make some arrangements for fishing at Salisbury.

He had himself feared that his lack of sight might keep him from holding office, and was not surprised that it debarred him from being in the Cabinet, but his friends were keenly disappointed. It was generally held at the time that his blindness was the cause of his exclusion, but it is noteworthy that Gladstone himself is not reported to have said so.

A contemporary newspaper wrote:

'No one asked why Mr. Fawcett was a member of the Government, but many inquired why he was not in the Cabinet. We have reason to believe that if Mr. Fawcett had been definitely apprised that his blindness was considered an insuperable barrier in the way of his admission to the Cabinet, he would have resigned office. He would not have consented to have been permanently debarred from the free discussion in Parliament of the questions in which he was intensely interested, and to which he brought a greater capacity of judgment than three-fourths of the members of any Cabinet England has ever seen. The opinions he could not express in council, he would have resumed the right of expressing in Parliamentary debate. It is a matter of regret that a barrier of weak prejudice should have excluded a man who had overcome so many real, and seemingly insuperable, barriers.'

It was argued that a member of the Cabinet has to see many confidential papers, and that there would be difficulty in admitting some one who, in order to read them, would have to use other eyes than his own. This explanation seems hardly sufficient. Six months later, Lord Hartington offered Fawcett a seat on the Indian Council, where confidential documents would also have to be scrutinised. The English Cabinet, even in its methods of procedure, is so secret, that it is impossible to dogmatise on the subject. But for that very reason, it seems the more plausible that difficulties such as those due to Fawcett's blindness could have been met and overcome. Fawcett's exclusion from the Cabinet may as much have been due to his uncompromising individuality as to his physical infirmity. It is to be remembered that Cabinet forming is difficult work, and a Prime Minister has to think of the claims and capacities of many candidates, and of how they will pull together. Furthermore, the principle that a man should serve in a subordinate office first, before being asked to join the Cabinet, was a favourite one with Gladstone.

FAWCETT'S SIGNATURE AND SEAL AS POSTMASTER GENERAL OF ENGLAND

The impression of the seal was taken from the actual seal used by Fawcett; but, at the time of King Edward's accession, when the expression "Her Majesty's" became incorrect, the word "his" was cut on the seal in substitution to the word "her"

The reader must draw his own conclusions as to these high matters of State. The only reference Fawcett is known to have made is in the letter to his father already quoted.

In a previous administration Gladstone had had reason to know that the financial work of a Postmaster-General is complex and full of intricate detail. In his choice of Fawcett for this post he showed his respect for the economist's financial ability. This respect was mutual: Fawcett in one of his letters speaks of 'the pleasure of doing business with a Master of the Art.'

On the spring day when Fawcett made his first call at the busy Post Office, he was warmly received by his predecessor and political opponent, Lord John Manners, and introduced by him to the leading officials.

An Official Welcome.

At a more formal reception to Fawcett, 'all the officials at the General Post Office' were mustered to be individually introduced to him, beginning with the heads of departments, with each of whom he shook hands. These were followed by officials next in rank. To the first of these Fawcett was about to hold out his hand, when the hint was whispered to him, 'It is not usual for Her Majesty's Post-master-General to shake hands with any one in the office below the rank of head of a department.'

Hand-shaking.

'I suppose,' rejoined Fawcett, 'that I am at liberty to make what use I like of my own hand,' and he went on shaking hands with every one who was presented to him.

There is a report that this democratic handshaking proclivity was shown also in the opposite direction socially. At some function when Royalty was present, Fawcett was sent for by the Queen. It was his first interview with her, and unlike a seeing man he had no chance to observe the customary etiquette in these matters. So he advanced cheerily, heartily grasped Her Majesty's hand and spoke of his pleasure in greeting her.

Queen Victoria always knew how to overlook an unintentional breach of etiquette, and fascinated, as so many were, by Fawcett's friendliness, chatted gaily and unceremoniously with him, while the court looked on, much amused and somewhat astounded.

A great Opening of Service.

To understand Fawcett's methods and the manner in which he took up his new work, it is essential to get his estimate of its scope, and of his relation to it as its director. His attitude was very simple. He was the servant of the people—an engine to lift their loads and to help them to help themselves to fuller, happier lives. He regarded the Post Office neither as an end in itself, nor as a money-making machine for the Government, but as an instrument which could be made of service, especially to the poor.

First, he wished to give the machine a *soul* and a heart: the thought of such things in the Post Office seems comic, but in Fawcett's time this miracle was accomplished. Its whole system was waked up, shaken from its lethargy, and flooded with a new interest, and that unusual *esprit de corps* which has been mentioned, was aroused among the employees, and alone made possible the results which he achieved.

As usual, far ahead of his time, he grasped the chief principles of scientific business management—that recent art which has claimed so much attention from the great capitalists and the directors of huge enterprises, especially in America. Without labelling his principles with high-sounding names, he carried them out, insisting on economy, both of work and fatigue, which produced contentment, increased interest and zeal among the employees; hence greater efficiency.

His method was, first, to diminish fatigue, perhaps the most wasteful factor in quasi-efficient business. Working and sanitary conditions were improved, and the staff of Post Office doctors was augmented. He noticed the failure in health, however slight, of those officers with whom he came in contact, and at once suggested that they should recruit themselves by leave of absence. Thus he raised the standard of physique among his workers. He tried to adjust the work to each individual. This seems impossible in so vast an enterprise, but by the tremendous amount of investigation which he made himself, and by seeing his humble employees as well as heads of departments, Fawcett brought this about to an astonishing degree. The threat of a strike among the telegraphists soon after he assumed office gave him an early opportunity to prove this. Fawcett investigated their grievances with much personal inquiry, and, by a re-classification of the employees, satisfactorily met their complaints.

Before long he had won the loyal adherence of the officials of his department, and it is delightful to see how highly he esteemed them and their integrity and industry. He was careful to give credit to the work of his subordinates, and to obtain for them any marks of approval or honorary distinctions that were their due. He would add to his own labours rather than cause a subordinate to be late for luncheon or lose a train home.

At that time the selection of women for Post Office work was not by open competition, but the applications were submitted to the Postmaster-General. Fawcett took much trouble about these, and would not allow himself to be affected by the influential backing of an applicant, but tried, other things being equal, to give the position to the one who needed it most.

The following interesting anecdote is told by Fawcett's old friend, Sir William Lee Warner: 'I remember on one occasion I passed him in the street in London, and he asked me to walk with him. First he asked me whether by chance any half-sovereigns had got into the pocket in which he kept sixpences. Then he wished to visit a certain Post Office, and as we went he would tell me his impressions of the names of the streets down which we passed, and ask me to correct him. His memory was wonderfully good, and even his sense of distances. "We must now be near such a post office," he said, and he was nearly always right. We entered it and I took him to the counter. "Is Miss B. here?" he asked. "No, but she will be back directly," was the reply. Then ensued a scene which impressed me with the inconvenience of blindness. Having ascertained that Miss B. was before him, he told her that he had received her application for promotion, and proceeded to discuss the matter with her. The applicant blushed greatly—her neighbours, and possibly her rivals, pressed forward to hear, and perhaps resent her application. The poor creature looked the more uncomfortable as the Postmaster-General became the more considerate and promised to give his best attention to her request.'

Help for Women.

Keen for any efficient service obtainable, he welcomed what able assistance women could offer. He largely extended the employment of women workers in the Post Office. This has proved so successful that the number of women in the various branches of the Post Office has steadily increased, and is now very large. Fawcett was wont to say that he considered the head of the women's staff of the Savings Bank one of the ablest officials in the whole postal service.

Mrs. Garrett Anderson, his sister-in-law, was deeply interested in his work for the women in the Post Office, and especially in his efforts to have them labour under healthful conditions. She was a distinguished doctor, and in 1882 Fawcett, after consultation with her, appointed a woman doctor to look after the women in the London post office. He also, with excellent results, appointed women doctors at Liverpool and Manchester. Under the improved conditions for health and of health, the women's work was eminently satisfactory, and at the time of his death there were two thousand nine hundred and nineteen employed in the department.

He noted that difficulties occurred when, as was then customary, on the marriage of a postmistress her appointment was given to her husband. When he was not the right person for the new place, this led to trouble; in 1882 the passage of the Married Woman's Property Act enabled him to decide that a woman should in every case have the option of retaining the appointment in her own name. This arrangement was confirmed by Lord Eversley, who succeeded Fawcett at the Post Office.

Fawcett went personally into many complaints against petty officials. Unless fully convinced, he was righteously unwilling to dismiss a man, and so often leave him with a stigma for life. Losses of letters having occurred in a local post office, a watch was set, and suspicion fell on a clerk who had been caught using telegrams for racing and betting. As a preliminary measure, the clerk was removed to another office for a month, and the irregularities immediately ceased; he was then sent back, and at once they began again. What could be a clearer case? He must be dismissed at once. 'Give him another chance,' said Fawcett. 'He has admitted his gambling. Had he denied it I should have been convinced he was guilty of thefts.' Certain tests, usual in the Post Office service, were applied, and the result proved conclusively that the culprit was a guard on the railway, who had been astute enough to forgo taking the letters during the absence of the suspected clerk, and who began again when the man returned. 'There, you see,' said Fawcett, 'by a little extra care I saved a foolish young man from the absolute ruin of character which his dismissal from the Post Office would have caused.'

Again we are reminded of his likeness to that other great, tall, contemporary champion of justice, who, across the Atlantic, had given his life to serve the oppressed and the debased. Lincoln's critics were always reproaching him for his excessive leniency and clemency; he would never let a shadow fall on the life of an unfortunate if he could help it. He forgot to sign the death warrant for a scared boy who had run away when his officer told him to face his first mad sight of battle; and he meekly granted a widowed mother a pardon for her renegade son. So Fawcett, in his peaceful rôle of directing the Post Office, hated and hesitated to confirm an order for dismissing a subordinate. His critics say that occasionally he pushed clemency to weakness, and that he was 'unwilling to enforce punishments really called for in the interests of the necessary discipline.' More than a quarter of a century has passed since this was said, and with the definition of bad (as good out of place) we have come to question the use of so-called punishments. Perhaps Fawcett and Lincoln, in trying not to inflict them, because of their dislike to give pain, were in this respect also far ahead of their time, and, by their intuitive hate of doing an injury to any one, were anticipating the wisest policy of to-day, which seeks by scientific adjustment and inspiration to do away with so crude a thing as punishment. The future will judge of this, but we can appreciate the righteous fear such men had of unjustly interfering with personal rights, or trying to make a stereotyped formula fit an erring human being.

When differences of opinion occurred, Fawcett would discuss the question with his subordinates to an 'almost wearisome length' because he disliked unnecessarily to thrust their opinions aside. He often said that as he could not see himself, he had an earnest wish to see things as much as possible from the point of view of others. By bringing home his personality to the great mass of Post Office servants, and by calling the attention of the public to the value of the work done by the permanent staff, he raised the tone of the whole service, enhanced their self-respect, and increased the estimation in which they are held by the public.

Esprit de Corps.

The employee who had fallen under the spell of his new chief's enthusiasm and kindliness felt, no matter how humble a niche he occupied, that he was doing part of the good work of a great country, and forgot that he was, perhaps, a poorly paid clerk in a God-forsaken hamlet. His efforts would be redoubled; the golden chain of service linked all the little outlying posts with the great ones, bound even the little half-frozen postmistress in the bleakest settlement of the empire to help on the work of the jovial, warm-hearted chief in the brilliant city of London.

CHAPTER XXVI

FRESH AIR, BLUE RIBBONS, AND POSTMEN

A Day with the Postmaster-General—How he worked Reform—The Parcel Post.

By his intense love of the open air Fawcett kept mind and body fresh, and was eager and able to cope with his problems, and to welcome new ones. The late Sir Robert Hunter said: 'He frequently walked up and down outside the post office in the middle of the day, while smoking his cigarette, and on Saturdays he either walked, or rowed on the Thames with an old friend or two. He rowed very badly, and caused much discomfort to his companions by 'catching crabs.'

'I often used to accompany him, on long walks over Wimbledon Common, and he liked walking on uneven ground as contrasted with smooth pavements. I remember his saying one day how much better it was to get out into the country than to follow the prevalent fashion of hanging about the clubs on a Saturday, on the chance of picking up some piece of political gossip, gossip mostly untrue and worthless.' It is also told that when a mutual friend mentioned to Fawcett that he was going to stay in the country with the newly appointed solicitor: 'Ah,' said the blind man, 'you are going down to ——: Hunter has a wonderful view there!'

Applications did not need to be influentially backed to receive his interested attention. The request of a cottager to have his letters brought to his own cottage instead of to the house of his employer would be investigated by Fawcett as carefully as a request from a Minister of State. Nothing was too much trouble for him. He received a petition from the town of Guildford asking for an additional daily postal delivery. He invited a small deputation from among the signers of the petition to come to London and talk the matter over with him. Among those who formed the deputation was a medical man who gave the following account of what took place at the interview: 'After Fawcett had welcomed us most kindly, he had a little map of the town, which had been specially drawn up for the occasion, distributed among us, and then himself gave us an address on the work of the Guildford postmen. He described minutely the various rounds of each of them, specifying the names of the streets passed through, and the length of time occupied in traversing them. Summing up these data, he proved that the additional delivery for which we asked could only be provided at the cost of engaging an additional postman, which the local finances would not justify. None of us had a word to say against this demonstration, and I, for my part, quitted the General Post Office filled with astonishment that a blind man should seem to know more than I myself did about a town in which, as boy and man, I had been going about all my life.'[3]

What kind of a Donkey?

A large factor in his success was that he always kept his sense of humour to the fore. A friend remonstrated with the Postmaster-General because the post was brought to him by a donkey. But his only answer was a deeply interested inquiry, 'What kind of a donkey is it, a lean donkey, or a fat donkey?'

Blue Ribbon.

When complaint was made to the Postmaster-General that it was not 'official' for women working in the Post Office to wear the 'blue ribbon,' Fawcett replied that by doing so they set a very good example, and he had no fault to find with their office work. To a similar complaint about a postman, he replied that they might wear all the colours of the rainbow if it would keep them from drinking.

Though he did not take part in the various temperance campaigns of his day, Fawcett believed very strongly in the evils of drink. His own temperate existence, the fact that even in his college days he had never drunk too much, put him in a strong position to talk to others about the foolishness of drunkenness and the great loss of strength caused by an indulgence in drink. He was much in earnest in trying to persuade men of all classes to be temperate, and would unhesitatingly argue with hard-drinking men against their unwise course.

A day with the Postmaster-General.

The following outline of his daily work is kindly given by Mr. Dryhurst, who was his secretary at the time. The official pouches would be brought to the House of Commons at six o'clock. These contained the 'minutes,' to use the official term, *i.e.* the proposals submitted for his approval or instructions. His secretary would get up these papers and afterwards read them to his chief. This had to be a thorough process, for Fawcett, instead of passing them as a matter of form, was certain to ask minute questions about them. He returned home from the House of Commons any time from one to four A.M. After breakfast the following morning, 'the meat,' as he called it, would be read to him out of the morning news, and then important papers would be put before him to be approved or initialled. If he felt he did not know enough to approve or disapprove, he would ask to see So-and-so later at the post office. At eleven-thirty to twelve, partly by cab and partly on foot, he would reach the post office, and there spend the next three to four hours in discussing with the officials the proposals they had put before him, or new ones which were in contemplation.

Other important business during the parliamentary session would be the preparation of answers to the questions to be asked in the House of Commons in the afternoon. As soon as this work was done, he walked along the Embankment from Blackfriars to the House of Commons.

---

[3] This account was given in approximately the above words by the late Mr. Henry Taylor of Guildford to his cousin, Mr. Sedley Taylor of Cambridge.

It is interesting to set beside this more impressions of Sir Robert Hunter, which he most kindly gave to the writer shortly before his death. Sir Robert was appointed solicitor to the Post Office by Fawcett, who was particularly glad to make the appointment, as Mr. Hunter, as he was then, was an old friend. The two men had worked together in the Commons Preservation Society, to which Sir Robert Hunter was the indefatigable solicitor, and Fawcett had then become thoroughly familiar with his great abilities.

How he worked.

Speaking of the blind Postmaster-General, Sir Robert said that he gave the Post Office an enormous lift; he tried to make it an important social instrument for the amelioration of the State. His personality was most inspiriting. He would come to the post office on Monday morning with a crumpled little piece of paper, which he would hand to any one standing near to read to him. It contained perhaps half a dozen words; for example: 'Foreign delivery, parcels, stamp, alterations.' This slight help to his memory was sufficient to remind him perhaps of all the day's work, including investigations and even what he was prepared to say before the House of Commons in the afternoon. He took great pains with his answers for question time, discussing, writing, and re-writing them. But once they were settled and read over to him in their final form, they were delivered by him in the House verbatim without any effort. If some proposal came before him in the guise of a file of papers, he always endeavoured to ascertain what official had given most consideration to the question, and he then discussed the matter with him personally. This was an innovation. The discussion would suggest ideas which would often lead to improvements in the administration. His enthusiasm made every one feel the need of working harder and doing better than under a less inspiring leader. He gained the affection of all by his astonishing consideration, and by not giving unnecessary trouble.'

Though now a mature and distinguished man, he had not changed from his buoyant earlier self, and with each return to Cambridge took up his lectures and his social life with a new glow and fresh zeal. He appreciated more than ever, if possible, the value of work and fun in life, and in return, for his industry and gaiety, life yielded him full measure of joy and contentment.

Interested Cows.

A Trinity Hall contemporary tells of going to stay with a friend in the country, and on his arrival finding no one at home; but being told by the butler that Mr. Fawcett had arrived and was fishing in the neighbourhood, the new guest went in search. After a short walk in the meadows he was surprised to see in the neighbourhood of a brook a large group of cows standing in contemplation about some central object which he could not make out. A nearer view revealed Fawcett seated in the charmed circle, the cynosure of all the bovine eyes! In his hand he held a fishing-rod, the line being firmly caught above his head to the branch of a tree. The anxious and puzzled observer asked what was the matter, to which Fawcett answered unconcernedly: 'Oh, I'm all right, thanks; I'm very glad to see you!' On further inquiry about his hypnotised audience of cows, he explained, 'Oh, it was the boy's lunch-time, so I sent him off to get it. My fish-hook got caught in the tree and these cows just happened to come round.' As always, he was having an idyllic time, and was amused by his friend's perplexity.

A Faithful Plaster.

Mr. Dryhurst tells of Fawcett in a different predicament, the centre of a very different circle at Cambridge. Like most healthy men, he took his trifling ailments most seriously, and was much worried by any unusual symptoms. One day, having a fearful pain in his chest, he went to a chemist in Cambridge. The chemist properly made inquiry as to a possible cause for the trouble. Had there been perhaps some reckless indulgence? some forbidden fruit or similar dissipation? Fawcett could find, however, no possible explanation for his illness, though he parenthetically remarked that he had eaten forty walnuts. The chemist finally prescribed for this mysterious illness a tar adhesive plaster and applied a large one to Fawcett's chest. The same evening the invalid went to a dinner-party. The weather was close, the room badly ventilated. A slight but rapidly increasing odour of tar was noticed by one or two of the guests. Fawcett blandly remarked that they were repairing the streets of Cambridge, which might perhaps account for the odour, and thus diverted any awkward investigation.

A German Visitor.

On his return to London, Fawcett was asked by the head of the German Post Office to allow him to send an official to study certain points of administration. Fawcett gladly gave the required leave, and on reaching the office one morning was informed that the German official had arrived and was already at work in one of the departments. 'Tell him,' said Fawcett, 'that I should be glad to speak to him in my room.' As a considerable time elapsed without his putting in an appearance, Fawcett asked the reason for the delay, and received the following answer: 'Directly we told the German gentleman that you wished to speak to him, he put on his coat and hat and left the office, and we saw him drive off in a hansom cab.' This seemed a very odd way of behaving, but the matter was satisfactorily cleared up before long by the return of the German visitor in full official costume and with all his orders on. Fawcett, concealing his amusement, expressed his regret that so much trouble should have been thrown away on a blind man who could not perceive the results. The German visitor explained that in no case could he have presented himself before a Minister of a foreign power in ordinary attire. To have done so would have rendered him liable to most serious censure from his own official superiors.

New Ideas.

Fawcett always lent a ready ear to all suggestions for widening the work. Friends told him of the reply postcard and of the indicators used abroad to show when the last collection had been made at the pillar boxes. Gleefully, like a boy with a new toy, he seized these, to him, new ideas, and made them part of the little details of his great machine. He loved to watch the effect of any new improvement, and was interested in hearing of the greater convenience and consequently greater correspondence due to the erection of a pillar box in Salisbury near his old home. He multiplied pillar boxes in railway stations, and had letter boxes fixed to the travelling post offices in trains, and greatly accelerated the collection and delivery of letters. He arranged for the issue of postal orders on board ship, and earned the gratitude of pensioners by arranging to have their money sent by post, thus saving them a journey. The official reports testify to his love of the minutiæ of his task.

Five things to be done.

He was as genuinely absorbed in it as if the administration of the Post Office had been the desire of his lifetime. In a letter to his father on 7th April 1883, he names briefly his chief ambitions for the extension of his work. He writes: 'Before I had been a fortnight at the Post Office I felt that there were five things to be done: (1) The parcel post; (2) the issue of postal orders; (3) the receipt of small savings in stamps and the allowing of small sums to be invested in the funds; (4) increasing the facilities for life insurance and annuities; (5) reducing the price of telegrams. The first four I have succeeded in getting done, and now the fifth is to be accomplished.'

Parcel Post.

It is only last year (1913) that the United States Post Office, after many struggles, has at last followed the example of the Mother Country in introducing the parcel post. At this time it may be of especial interest to take a short survey of the history of this great agent for helpfulness and of the splendid part which Fawcett played in promoting it. As early as 1698 Docwra originated the penny post for London. It dispensed impartially 'bank boxes, tradesmen's parcels, and apothecaries' mixtures.' Patients complained wisely or unwisely (for it seems that there has always been a faction in favour of mind cure) that they did not get their physic in time. But the high rate of postage put an end to this. Though a parcel post was advocated by Sir Rowland Hill, the Society of Arts, the Royal Commission on Railways, and though Lord John Manners had opened up negotiations with the various interests involved, no working agreement had been arrived at. When Fawcett took office he became keenly interested and persisted resolutely till the many difficulties were overcome. It required tireless patience, tact, and diplomacy, both with the Treasury department, which had to provide funds to meet the first outlay, and with the railway companies. Fawcett's part in the work of establishing this new system was interrupted by illness, but, nevertheless, the new order was in full swing in August 1883.

The new red Vans.

He took a keen delight in this fresh work, of which he felt that the public should have the benefit, even if the Government made little profit. On the evening when the parcel post was started, Fawcett, with his wife and daughter, went to the 'circulation office.' He writes afterwards on the same night to his parents, describing the scene, the extraordinary variety of objects posted, and the 'smartly painted red vans.' He begs them to come and have a look at it. Three days later he reports that things are working smoothly, and speaks warmly of the zeal of all concerned, from the head officials down to the humblest letter-carrier. He says that he shall soon issue a general notice of thanks to the persons co-operating in the result. The only difficulty was the public inexperience in the art of packing.

In his report Fawcett writes: 'The new post had been introduced without the least interference with the older services. The number of parcels conveyed had increased and was now at the rate of from twenty-one to twenty-two millions a year. Simplifications, and consequent economies had been introduced, and further improvements were under consideration.'

PUNCH, OR THE LONDON CHARIVARI.——April 15, 1882.

THE MAN FOR THE POST.

With special permission from the Proprietors of "Punch"

Though not at first a financial success, the parcel post became a great national asset, and later also a generous contributor to the national exchequer; and though Fawcett's death came too soon, probably, for him to realise the quick improvement, his innovations and model methods made the English Post Office an all-important study for other countries.

The Heart of the Post Office.

Men, not things, interested Fawcett, as they do most born leaders. He knew that if he could energise the minds and bodies of the men and women of the peaceful army he commanded, and fill them with zeal for their job, the work of England's Post Office would go of itself. The machinery would fly, and each department fill its mission with miraculous new life. Telegrams, letters, and parcels would dart and fly with fresh quickness to their destinations, and the revenue from his latest ventures would return, like a carrier pigeon, to his fostering hand.

Fawcett's magnetism and good nature, combined with his driving energy, and his love for the work and the workers, brought about the transformation of the Post Office from a partially efficient machine to a highly sensitive, highly organised, democratic department, highly efficient for the good of his country and its dependencies. His irrepressible enthusiasm for service infected his force from the lowest to the highest, brought out the best in them, and knit them together by this bond of interest and brotherhood. He instilled in them the fervour for conquest of the nobler kind that inspires patriots, soldiers, or explorers. Thus he gave wings, interest, even poetry to the stamping of letters and collecting of mail.

CHAPTER XXVII

THE PENNIES OF THE POOR

Cheap Postal Orders—Savings Bank—Life Insurance—Two Post Office Pamphlets to help the People—Cheap Telegrams—Telephones—'The Man for the Post'—'Words are Silver, Silence is Gold.'

Postal Money Orders.

It had been felt for some time that it would be possible to send small sums of money by post more cheaply. The only method, that of Post Office Money Orders, in force when Fawcett became Postmaster-General, was well described by him when he said: 'If a boy wanted to send his mother the first shilling he had saved, he would have to pay twopence for the order and a penny for postage.' A committee had a measure prepared to remedy this, and Fawcett quickly saw its value and got the measure passed through Parliament. Thus originated the Postal Order which is so familiar to us all.

Postal Savings Bank.

In making this change Fawcett had to overcome the opposition of the banking interest, who considered that the Government was infringing on their preserves. He came into conflict with them again when he increased the facilities of the Savings Bank. He made it possible to begin with the smallest sums by adopting the scheme of stamp slip deposits, which had been worked out and devised by Mr. Chetwynd, an official of the Post Office. This was a blank form which could be filled up with twelve penny stamps, and then deposited in the Savings Bank.

At this time Fawcett, with the help of a Mr. Cardin, another official, prepared his first popular pamphlet, called 'Aids to Thrift.' He took an enormous amount of interest in this little leaflet, which he felt would be a great help to the poor and ignorant. He tried to give the information printed in the regular Post Office Guide in the simplest language, so that the benefits offered by the Post Office could be easily grasped by the most ignorant.

The Working Man who Insured.

A sad incident set his mind to working out another scheme for lessening the difficulties of the working man. 'A poor neighbour employed in a mill near Salisbury had fallen ill. He had insured himself in a certain society which was to pay him an allowance in case of illness. The allowance was stopped under certain pretences strongly suggestive of fraud. Fawcett, to whom he appealed, immediately called at the offices of the society. The secretary, not recognising his visitor, treated him with considerable insolence. Fawcett brought the man to his senses, extracted certain sums from the society, and took steps to investigate the nature of its business. He had the satisfaction of obtaining something for the poor man, who died not long afterwards. Fawcett did what he could for the family.'

PUNCH OR, THE LONDON CHARIVARI—November 27, 1880.

THE NEW STAMP DUTY.

Mr. Fawcett. "NOW, THEN, ALL OF YOU, 'IN FOR A PENNY IN FOR A POUND.'"

"Mr. Fawcett's scheme brings saving within everybody's reach." —Times.

With special permission from the Proprietors of "Punch"

Post Office Annuities.

The facts which he gleaned in connection with this case and others, as well as from his many friendships since childhood with labourers and peasants, made him realise the problems which beset the poor who wish to insure against the future. He improved the system of Post Office Annuities, and arranged for the publication of a short paper called 'Plain Rules for the Guidance of persons wishing to make provision for the future with the aid of the Government.' This also was to be had gratuitously, and did much to teach the poor how to provide for themselves.

Cheaper Telegrams.

Fawcett regretted that telegrams were too expensive to be a convenience for any but the rich. The betting ring and the Stock Exchange were its principal patrons. He was deeply interested in lowering the cost, so that telegrams could become useful to the 'plain people.' Among the first deputations to be given an audience by the new Postmaster, was one requesting cheap telegrams. He set himself with a will to get them, writing and speaking to urge this new reform. It meant a fresh expense for the Treasury, at least at the beginning, and he could not get the consent of that department. But there were many members of the House of Commons who favoured the change, and pushed it, relying on the Postmaster-General's well-known sympathy. In 1883 they succeeded in outvoting the Government, and the adoption of sixpenny telegrams became certain.

The Telegraph Boys.

Fawcett always had a fellow-feeling for the small boy, and he was very anxious that the telegraph boys used in the Post Office should be kept in the service, mounting from their positions as understudies of Mercury to those of greater distinction and better pay. When on a visit to a friend in a suburb of a large manufacturing town, Fawcett found that his friend was able by telephone to direct his business in the town by half an hour's conversation, and was then free for the rest of the day. This so greatly impressed Fawcett, that he became eager to give the public as large an enjoyment of telephones as possible. He was in favour of granting the widest possible liberty to qualified persons to start telephone exchanges, making the condition that the Post Office should be paid a royalty of ten per cent., and that no written telephone messages should be delivered. One of his last acts was the approval of a licence containing these terms, which was signed by his successor. He refused firmly but gently, in his last interview at the Post Office, to grant to a gentleman the protection which he asked for a small telephone company, thus showing himself to the last true to his belief in open competition.

An Executive Genius.

We have now seen something of Fawcett's task at the Post Office, thirty-three years ago, and how he strove to do the work largely in accordance with our most approved and up-to-date methods. Some of his tools are now obsolete, the work has been changed in detail, but the philosophy and wisdom, the business sense and control which he showed in his four and a half years of office were what could be considered to-day so remarkable, so successful, as to amount to executive genius.

Sir Arthur Blackwood, who was Permanent Secretary to the Post Office in Fawcett's day, used of his chief this striking phrase: 'He had a passion for justice.' His only criticism of Fawcett's administration was that he was too lenient to erring subordinates, and apt to give too much time to details which might have been entrusted to others. His conclusion was: 'The Post Office could never, I believe, have a more capable Postmaster-General, nor its officers a truer friend.'

As witness to this last, a post-office clerk wrote: 'The humblest servant within the dominion of his authority was not left uncared for. During his history as Postmaster-General, a greatly improved state of feeling has been introduced among the officers in their general tone towards each other and towards those beneath them.'

The view of the country at large was equally emphatic. Let these verses from *Punch*, written after Fawcett had been two years in office, speak for the popular appreciation of his work:—

'THE MAN FOR THE POST

JOHN BULL *loquitur*

Well, well, here's comfort, and, by Jove, it's needed
Amidst the chaos of cantankerous cackle,
Here is one man has silently succeeded—
One man who a tough job can stoutly tackle.
O si sic omnes! In my blatant Babel
Business is a lost art—at least it seems so.
All the more honour to the Champion able
Who still can realise my hopes and dreams so,
To serve the State, to sagely shape and plan for it,
Is the true Statesman's part, and here's the man for it.

No epic hero! Well, I'm getting weary
Of the huge windiness now dubbed heroic,
"Arms and the Man"—and a fiasco dreary
Too oft repeated, irritate a Stoic
Such as I'm grown. And then I'm not quite certain,
Applied to him the name *is* pure misnomer.
Fawcett, though seldom called before the curtain,
Perhaps in more than *one* point pairs with *Homer*.
Although one sang Achilles and his host,
The other schemed, not sang, the Parcels Post.

Perhaps the large ambition that loves spangles
And warrior fame might pooh-pooh the projectors,
But I'm inclined to fancy Red Tape's tangles
Are tougher foes than many Trojan Hectors.
Achilles as Laocoön might have thundered
And thrust tremendously, and yet been throttled.
St. Stephen's spouters long have fought and blundered,
And long my rising wrath I've choked and bottled,

> But I *am* glad to see one silent, strong fellow,
> Who emulates the hero sung by Longfellow.
>
> "Something attempted, something done!" Precisely!
> A friend of mine, who much inclined to scoff is,
> Declares when Fawcett's plans have ripened nicely,
> The World will be a branch of the Post Office.
> Let the Wit wag, the World won't find salvation
> In parcels or reply-cards, stamps or thriftiness;
> Danger there may be in "centralisation,"
> But after all the squabbling, hobbling shiftiness
> Of the cantankerous, rancorous jaw-jaw-jaw-set,
> 'Tis a relief to turn to turn to Henry Fawcett!'

The 'one silent, strong fellow' had learned a patience and tact in his later years that stood him in good stead when he found himself member of a Government, and there bound to refrain from criticising its actions. A story told of him at this time shows a gentle avoidance of differences not so common in his earlier days.

Professor Clifford, an old Cambridge friend, and secretary of the whilom Republican Club, died in 1880 leaving his widow in straitened circumstances. Professor Clifford was a mathematician of the first order, but, especially in his later years, he became an aggressive anti-religionist, and wrote much on these matters.

A Widow's Pension.

Fawcett wanted to arrange for a pension for the widow, and took occasion to speak to the Prime Minister. Gladstone took Fawcett with him down to his room and asked him, 'Who is the great man at Cambridge now?' Fawcett mentioned the loss that the university had recently sustained by the death of its mathematician, carefully alluding to Professor Clifford in this manner. Gladstone said, 'I always regarded him as a third-rate theologian.' To which Fawcett said, 'I know nothing about his theology, but as a mathematician he stood in the very front rank.' This opinion of Fawcett's so impressed Gladstone that Mrs. Clifford's name was added to the Civil Pension List.

Fawcett would not have joined the Ministry unless he felt in real sympathy with its avowed principles, but it is probable that had he remained independent he would have found much to criticise. Leslie Stephen comments: 'His position as a Minister without a seat in the Cabinet imposed reserve, whilst it did not enable him to exert any direct influence upon the Government. On some points I can only conjecture his probable views. Mr. Gladstone's Government was especially notable for its Irish and Egyptian policy. In both cases I imagine Fawcett's sympathy must have been imperfect.'

This position requiring silence, without giving him power to exert direct influence on the Government, must have been, to one of his frank, honest, fighting temperament, at times very difficult.

Interest in Ireland.

He was profoundly interested in Ireland, and felt that the only satisfactory symptom in Irish matters was the increased use of the Savings Bank. A friend of Fawcett's having casually mentioned his name in a remote part of Ireland, was surprised at the exclamation, 'Oh, we know all about him here!' This remark was based on the fact that a girl from the district had gone with great credit through all the stages of a telegraph clerk's position in the English General Post Office. On her quitting to get married, Fawcett had sent for her, and in the kindest manner thanked her for her past services, and offered his hearty good wishes for her happiness.

April 9, 1861.] PUNCH, OR THE LONDON CHARIVARI. 159
"HERE STANDS A POST!"
With special permission from the Proprietors of "Punch"

He felt strongly that exceptional legislation was required to deal with the land questions of Ireland, and that any legislation would be futile which did not reflect in some way the wishes of the Irish themselves. No one could be more opposed than he to Home Rule, which, he declared, meant 'the disruption of the Empire.' He would rather, as he said on one occasion, that the Liberal Party should remain out of office till its youngest member had grown grey with age, than be intimidated into voting for Home Rule. Still he held that some such legislation as that embodied in Mr. Gladstone's Land Bill was necessary.

It is related that once at this time, when sitting with friends who were discussing the Irish irreconcilability, he kept repeating, as if to himself, 'We must press on and do what is right'; and he wrote to his father, 'There is nothing for it, but to persevere in doing justice in spite of all provocation.'

Loyal Work and Loyal Silence.

He felt that the Egyptian policy was weak, and on one or two occasions so far showed his distrust as to refuse to vote. But for the most part he absorbed himself in the work of his own department, and did it nobly. He gave hard work, sound sense, resolute purpose, and a gay elasticity of spirit which no weariness could break. It was truly said of him that he bettered everything and kept his eye on everything. In this, as in every task, he neared his ideal which he had expressed on leaving Cambridge: 'To exert an influence in removing the social evils of our country, and especially the paramount one, the mental degradation of millions. I regard it as a high privilege of God if He will enable me to assist in such a work.'

A TRIUMPHANT END

'Strive for the truth unto death, and the Lord shall fight for thee.'
'The things which are seen are temporal, but the things which are unseen are eternal.'

CHAPTER XXVIII

AT HOME AND AT COURT

Appreciating Opponents—Hackney Address—Proportional Representation—Justice for Women—A State Concert—Humble Friendships—Pigs—Salisbury again.

Appreciating Opponents.

The same respect for the individuality of others which made Fawcett unwilling to punish a subordinate if he could honourably avoid it, which made him often detect good qualities in the offender to compensate for the offence, made him also quick to respect and admire an adversary, even when strongly repudiating his principles. Fawcett never forgot that his opponent was a human being, however different their political creeds. In his later years his sympathy may not have been any deeper than in his vigorous youth, but it expressed itself more gently and more skilfully. When his fine wrath was roused, he still had at his command barbed arrows of sarcasm and thunders of denunciation, but his speech was more apt to be kindly. He trusted more than in his less experienced days to force of example and to irrefutable logic. His fairness and justice stood out in fine contrast to the hectic verbal warfare raging between rival factions. When, on 13th October 1884, he spoke in public for the last time, he administered a grave rebuke to 'the spirit of mutual intolerance,' saying:

'Prudence and Patriotism.'

'If we take a calm review of the situation ... we refuse to enter into useless recriminations and taunts about the past. I still have not relinquished the hope ... that the counsels of common sense, prudence, and patriotism will prevail.... Can we come to any other conclusion than that the present is a time when the dictates of prudence and patriotism demand that everything should be done to lessen, rather than to intensify, the bitterness of party strife.'

He went on to speak on a subject which had been much in his mind from the beginning of his political career. Proportional representation meant to him the method, and the only method, by which the different elements of the body politic could be fairly represented in Parliament. So earnestly did he hold to this view that he made up his mind, with his friend Lord Courtney, to resign his office should the Government proceed with legislation incompatible with these principles. In this last word on a subject on which it has been necessary in this book to omit so many other words, Fawcett emphasised the main principle in these phrases: 'While we regard it as of the first moment that no important section of opinion should be effaced from representation, yet at the same time we are most anxious to secure to the majority the preponderance of power to which it is justly entitled. Let the voice of the weak be heard as well as the voice of the strong by your Government, give fair play to all, and make justice possible.' And he added this vital remark: 'The enfranchisement of women, already dictated by justice, would soon become a necessity.'

Fawcett's unfailing Chivalry.

His unfailing chivalry was always a radiant characteristic of his courteous nature, and he felt it his high privilege to serve women; he had the faculty of encouraging them, and filling them with confidence in their own ability; his voice, though not melodious, had a peculiar brightness that raised drooping spirits, and impressed itself upon the memory. Besides the encouragement which he gave by the employment of women in the Post Office, his efforts for compulsory education, now accepted as a matter of course, his labours to protect young children at work in factory or field, as well as his fight for free playgrounds and commons, were all helpful to the mothers of the race.

On the day after his death, a poor woman, who came to the employment office to make inquiries on behalf of her daughter, who wished to enter the Civil Service, must have expressed the feelings of hundreds of struggling women, when she said: 'We do not know who will help us now that so good a friend has gone.'

Fair-play Expedient.

Believing that justice must infallibly become the most expedient policy, he felt it was not only repugnant, but bad diplomacy, that any class should be excluded by force or prejudice from having a voice in the Government, and he realised to the full that government could only be fair when it existed with the consent of the governed.

The constant society of his wife and other brilliant women of her family and her friends, impressed him with the great benefit that it would be to the community to have the assistance of their votes, as expressing their fair and able minds. He said concerning women's voting: 'The Parliamentary suffrage should be applied to those women who fulfil the qualifications of property and residence demanded from the elector. That is to say, if a widow or a spinster is in possession of a house, and pays rates and taxes, she should have the borough vote, and if she possesses freehold or leasehold property, she should have a county vote, as if it were held by a man.'

The Uses of Adversity.

We have dwelt on the great part that Fawcett's blindness played in forming his character. It intensified his bravery and determination, broadened his sympathies, sharpened his observation, made his memory keener, quickened his intellect, and gave him a greater power to conquer himself and others. Affliction had given him strength as of steel well tempered, to withstand and pierce all muddled thought and murky sentiment, and so make the clear under-light of his soul a shining beacon to all who knew him. But there were, inevitably, quiet moments, when, all efforts unavailing, his blindness must have weighed heavily upon him. Seated by his fireside, feeling the glow which he might never see, he would listen to the crackling of the coal and the ticking of the clock as it marked a minute less of his darkness. Such hours had to be fought through single-handed, by his own courage and strength of will.

Hearth and Home.

No small part of his triumph over circumstance was due to the great affections and friendships which were at the heart of his life. Chiefest and most constant of these were his flawless devotion to his wife and daughter, and the singularly beautiful sympathy and companionship which he found at home. It is not for the biographer to intrude into this holy of holies—enough to know that Fawcett had with his wife that perfect understanding and fellowship, that entire sympathy and intellectual inspiration, which, when he was most sorely tried, gave him a sure haven of rest and happiness from which to start forth again, better armed and braver, to battle anew.

When Mrs. Fawcett was absent, her husband would postpone a decision of great moment until he was able to get her opinion. She often acted as his secretary, and in all matters was his trusted counsellor. In later years, his daughter Philippa, whose great talent was a source of deep interest to him, completed with her brilliant intellect and happy wit this perfectly attuned trio. There is a poetic justice that Fawcett having fought so for the admission of women students at Cambridge, it was left for his daughter to achieve the highest mathematical honours bestowed on any woman in Great Britain, when as a student at Newnham she won four hundred marks above the Senior Wrangler.

A blithe Spirit.

He still greatly enjoyed society, and threw himself so thoroughly into the spirit of sociability and gaiety, that he seemed to leave his critical Parliamentary self. Mrs. Fawcett, as a comment on his whole-souled capacity for finding all things and everybody lovely, jestingly composed this epitaph for him: 'Here lies the man who found every soup delicious and every woman charming.' He did, and what is more, he tried to make every one else find life lovely and to have as glorious a time as he did.

He would never overlook any quiet mousy individuals lost in the general gaiety, but would take pains to draw them out, to throw himself so thoroughly into their interests that he put them at their ease, and made them take part in the conversation and shine unwontedly.

A contemporary gives a gay glimpse of him chatting and joking merrily among the smart crowd at Lady Granville's. His tall figure towered over the little knot of friends invariably gathered round him.

A State Concert.

Fawcett duly attended the levees and occasional official dinners held by the Prince of Wales, and on one occasion, when in the neighbourhood of Balmoral, he dined with the Queen. With his wife he went to the concerts given by her at Buckingham Palace. These were very stately events. Arrayed in his court uniform, Fawcett would drive with his wife betimes to the palace; as they approached, the music of the band in the courtyard was in full swing, and they liked to hear it as they waited in line until the preceding carriages had deposited their burdens. The guests moved through the glass doors to the entrance-hall, which echoed the rumbling of wheels and the closing of the carriage doors, the clanging of the spurs and swords of the men. They mounted the main staircase between the stationed Yeomen of the Guard, Fawcett's cheery voice and laughter resounding as he greeted friends above and below him. A moment's pause on the threshold of the great concert-room, and here the parquet floor gave back the tapping of little slippered feet and the heavy tread of the men, as the groups of guests flocked together or dispersed to find places before the music began.

On both sides of the room were raised tiers of seats for the company. At one end was the low platform with chairs arranged for Royalty. At the opposite end, a balcony with the organ provided places for the singers and musicians. Crystal chandeliers with hanging stalactites lighted the brilliant scene. Fawcett's fine ear caught the tiny tinkle of the crystals, as they answered to the draughts from the movement of the crowd, or trembled when the waves of music shook them on their little metal moorings. The good acoustics of the room, and the consequent clearness of all the sounds, brought the scene with unusual vividness before the blind man.

Enter Victoria Regina et Imperatrix.

A sudden expectant murmur rose from the crowd, a pause, a flutter of silks and a tapping of scabbards, the organ played 'God save the Queen,' and the mighty little Empress entered and greeted her guests. Returning her courtesy, the brilliant throng bowed as a field of wheat swayed by the wind, until the Queen had seated herself in the centre of the dais, surrounded in due order by members of the Royal Family.

Then the guests resumed their places and the music began.

Voices of Youth and Art.

Here Fawcett, as much if not more than any other guests, enjoyed the fresh young voices of the chorus of young girls from the Royal School of Music, and choir-boys from the Chapel Royal. This youthfulness contrasted charmingly with the more formal and perfect singing of the great artists of whose skill Queen Victoria was so appreciative.

When the programme was finished, the Queen rose and, preceded by gentlemen of the court walking backwards, went to the supper-room, through an aisle formed by her guests, stopping as she passed the balcony, to speak to the chief artists. The princesses who followed her often darted a smile or stole a fleeting word with one of the throng, and the more decorous ladies-in-waiting brought up the rear of the procession. The guests followed, with them Fawcett guided by his wife.

As Royalty was well separated by an encircling wall of court gentlemen, the assault by the guests on the sandwiches, cakes and bonbons began without restraint. A horseshoe buffet surrounded the room. The throng stood about chatting together, waited upon by gorgeous footmen resplendent in scarlet and white. The clinking of glass and china was drowned in the general conversation, all the more lively after the long silent listening to the music. Then the guests drifted in friendly groups down to the great hall, where the names of departing guests called from footman to footman echoed among the pillars.

A frequent and happy conversation this, as they sat on the long benches, muffled up and waiting for their carriages, and doubtless more than one of Fawcett's good stories was cut short by the call 'The Postmaster-General's carriage stops the way.'

A Big Friend of all the World.

Though he could find amusement in any form of social intercourse, it was the opportunities of close companionship that he most valued. He rarely lapsed into silence, and with his family, when there were no guests at table, he would talk with the same animation as if he had been at a brilliant dinner. Talk was an essential of life to him; wherever he went, reserve vanished.

If any unsuccessful schoolmate, who had no other claim on him, wrote for help, he was always sure to get it. In his interviews he was marvellously patient, would never let a person leave him in anger or displeasure; few people left him without being his friends. If he said a sharp thing to any one, he confessed at once, and was not happy until he had made full amends; any irritable action towards another on his part caused him much more suffering than he inflicted.

His real democratic feeling and disregard of rank put him at his ease with all classes, his abounding geniality and accessibility often placed him in difficult predicaments from which it required a lively ingenuity successfully to extricate himself.

Once while he was walking, a well-known bore buttonholed the Postmaster-General, and explained at length how the Post Office might be regenerated. Fawcett listened patiently for five minutes; then when it was clear that the man had no idea or facts to offer, but only words, Fawcett held out his hand, saying, 'Good day, Mr. J— —, I am much obliged to you for your kind wish to help me,' and walked on, leaving the bore, who felt himself just warming to his work, helplessly stranded.

His Dog.

His servants and his friends loved him; he was wonderfully considerate to all dependants, and indeed to every one whom he met. Certainly he was over-attentive to his dog Oddo, who had emerged from a refuge of lost dogs to assume the high office of watch-dog in the garden of the London house. Fawcett was deeply interested in the higher education of this humble friend, and their common affection was very warm.

Sudden Friendships.

His friendships were so sudden, at times so instantaneous, that their strength and duration was surprising. He had an incredible number of people whom he called in all sincerity his intimate friends, and, as one of them says, 'all the overgrowth of new friendship seemed rather to strengthen than to stifle the earlier ties.' As we have recorded, even the voice of an acquaintance once made, was to him unforgettable. When walking in London with his sister, Fawcett met the Primate of New Zealand, who had been at Cambridge with him. They had not met for many years, and the Primate did not wish to trouble Fawcett by recalling a long-ago acquaintanceship. But Miss Fawcett, recognising him, stopped, and as soon as the Primate spoke, Fawcett exclaimed with delight, 'Why, it's Nevill!'

Postmaster and Pigs.

At Salisbury he invariably called on his father's old farm servant, Rumbold. Rumbold was one day giving to Fawcett's mother the last news from his sties, and he added 'Mind you tell Master Harry when you write to him, for if there's one thing he cares about, 'tis pigs.' Truly it was one thing, though it is generally suspected that the Postmaster had other interests.

His increased income as Postmaster-General made no change in his simple mode of life, though he may have spent a little more on riding; he had, however, the satisfaction of being able to buy his family more presents, and he took an intense delight in tactfully giving many little things; he heard his sister say that she very much liked a lamp by which she had read to him in London. To her surprise and delight, on her return to Salisbury its twin appeared, found and sent to her by her brother.

Nothing gave him greater pleasure than to have his parents and sister under his roof, and to give them a good time. One of the most touching things in his life was his intense affection for his father. When the father grew old and was forced to breakfast in bed, the big son, after saying good-bye to him in the morning, would often quickly run upstairs again just to kiss the old gentleman a second time.

Presents and Parents.

When his sister told him that his letters gave his parents the greatest pleasure of their lives, he never let a week elapse without sending off two newsy documents to Salisbury. These letters abound in affection and in many little proofs of his eagerness to make them happy. He sends a birthday present, a comfortable pair of 'Norwegian slippers,' or encloses letters containing bits of political news which he is at liberty to show them; he tells them of his triumphs, even of compliments which he thinks that they would like to hear, and boasts of the admiration expressed for his father's remarkable vigour and youthfulness for his years; he also compliments the admirable packing evinced by the excellent condition in which sundry gifts in various interesting hampers have arrived.

He ran down to Salisbury whenever he could make time, and was there for the ovation given by the Liberals to his father on his ninety-first birthday. The old gentleman had been a fighter in the Liberal ranks since the days of the great Reform Bill.

Six months later, in spite of the urgent claims Cambridge lectures and Post Office work made upon him, he again went to speak at Salisbury. Parliament was in session too, an unusual thing in November, so that he was particularly hard worked. Still November 17th found him at Salisbury speaking to an enthusiastic audience, of which his father was one. After the meeting he seemed exhausted, but he returned to London on the 20th, lectured at Cambridge on the 22nd, and on the 23rd discharged his business at the House of Commons.

CHAPTER XXIX

A GRAVE ILLNESS

Illness—Convalescence—Musical Discrimination.

He was suffering from a cold, and complained of feeling ill. Mrs. Fawcett had been called away by the fatal illness of her cousin. When she returned to London, it was to hear that her husband's illness was pronounced to be diphtheria, and it was rendered more serious later by typhoid and other complications.

Through the Valley and Back.

Until the end of December his condition was grave. During the first stage of the illness he had frequently been delirious, and remembered little of what had happened. His mind was made up that he would not recover, and he insisted on hearing the bulletins. They were read to him with omissions.

There was to be an important election at Liverpool, and he, remembering its date, asked about the prospect. It was his habit at Christmas to send to a list of country labourers whom he knew, or whose names had been given to him by his father, envelopes each containing a card on which was written 'Please give to bearer John Smith [so many] pounds of beef or mutton.' With the card he sent a personal letter after this fashion: 'Dear John, I enclose a ticket for Christmas beef. Hoping you and the children are well, I am,' etc. The entire list of these benefactions he kept clearly in his mind. Before he was out of his delirium, he asked his secretary to send out the Christmas letters and food tickets as usual.

A little later, when he was just beginning to recover, a Cambridge crony was permitted to stand for a short time by his bedside. In the midst of his own weakness, Fawcett's thoughts flew to a Cambridge friend in trouble, and he charged his guest to do the utmost to give whatever help was possible.

The course of Fawcett's illness was watched with extraordinary anxiety. It was the dominant theme at working men's meetings and in third-class railway carriages. The Royal Family showed the same interest as the labourers who discussed the latest bulletin in the market-place of Salisbury. The Queen telegraphed for news, at times twice a day. Gradually the patient improved, and the danger was pronounced over.

Convalescing with Vanity Fair.

The convalescent was permitted to see his friends, who in relays read to him the whole of *Vanity Fair*. After three weeks' inaction, he was allowed to write to his parents, and amidst great rejoicing the cat and dog were permitted to resume their usual place in the family circle. In the early part of January he went to stay at his father-in-law's, on the Suffolk coast.

His friend Mr. Sedley Taylor came to play to him. Fawcett would listen to him often for an hour at a time. Though he had little acquaintance with music, he showed for it a genuine appreciation and discrimination. There were two compositions which he particularly enjoyed, one by Mendelssohn and one by Bach, which Mr. Taylor often played in that sequence. One day, however, he inverted the order. After listening with interest, Fawcett remarked: 'I don't know how it is, Taylor, but somehow that Bach seems to have taken the taste out of the Mendelssohn.'

Visits he enjoyed.

At the end of this visit, Fawcett sent for all the servants, so that he might personally give each a gratuity and shake of the hand, while thanking them individually for the kindness they had shown him. When no more were forthcoming, Fawcett said: 'Where is that boy that blacks the shoes? I should like to give him a tip too.' Whereupon the boy, who had been overlooked, was sent for and duly rewarded.

Fawcett went on to pay some other visits in the west of England, which seemed to help him regain his strength. It was at this time that he first successfully amused himself by playing cards, though his former attempts had been so unpromising. His secretary devised the simple and ingenious method of marking the cards, which has been described, so that he could tell each one by touch. Thus he was able with great satisfaction to spend hours at cribbage, écarté and loo.

In February he went to stay with his parents at Salisbury, and there used his enforced leisure to prepare a new edition of his book on Political Economy. It was there that a stranger to the town, not knowing his way, questioned a tall scholarly man who approached briskly. He was given minute directions; the streets and their windings were described in detail, and it was only after an amusing chat that the stranger discovered that his guide was the learned Professor Fawcett, and that therefore he must be blind! It was extraordinary how his own attitude to his affliction caused others to forget it. Not infrequently his cottage friends would tidy up and put things in order 'in case Mr. Fawcett should drop in.'

With his Parents again.

It was a great joy to his old parents in the Salisbury Close to have their busy, cheery 'boy' back again; and Miss Fawcett, that brave understanding friend in his affliction and throughout his life, was very happy in his companionship. One day they had been talking together as only those who have always understood each other can, lovingly they had gone over reminiscences of Salisbury and Cambridge, and had fought Parliamentary battles over again. Fawcett told his sister that above all his other work, he cherished his privilege of winning the forests and commons free for the people, theirs to the end of time.

His Sister and the Cathedral.

The two sauntered together into the near-by cathedral where, as a tiny, half-scared boy, Harry had gone clinging to his big sister's hand. Now the tall blind man held her arm, and his cane on the pavement was echoed by the high arches; suddenly a great glory of music broke forth from the organ, magic uplifting notes shook the walls, and piercing with gladness the shadows of centuries, rehallowed the old sanctuary with melody. Fawcett stood leaning slightly against a column, his heroic head uplifted as if he were looking through the vaulting, his whole being suffused with an inward light, and his sensitive ear revelling in the lovely harmonies. The voices of men and women raised in chorus burst forth in a mighty Hallelujah; the organ thrilled in glorious fulness, and again the voices repeated the refrain until it echoed from the wall like a song of triumph of good over evil, of light over darkness. A glad smile broke over the blind man's face as, pressing his dear companion's hand, he exclaimed: 'Oh, how beautiful that is!'

Back to his Post.

He returned to his work in March, seemingly in fully restored health.

His reception at the Post Office and the House of Commons showed how deep had been the love and anxiety called forth by his illness. He lived in the hearts of all classes—his bitterest antagonists, Conservatives as well as Socialists, loved and trusted him; never was a man more of a democrat and less of a demagogue.

Humble friends.

The old woman who for many years had the care of Fawcett's rooms at Cambridge had been much distressed by his illness, and had said to the Master of Trinity Hall, 'Poor Mrs. Fawcett would miss him so terribly.' 'Why should she miss him more than any woman would miss the husband she loved?' sympathetically asked the Master. 'Because he is such a happy noisy man; whenever he is in the house you know it, he is always shouting so,' was the tearful reply.

A poor old shoemaker who had never spoken to Fawcett, but whose shop the Postmaster-General passed daily on his way to his work, gave voice to the public feeling when he said, 'If Professor had died, I should have missed him dreadfully. He always looked so pleased and cheery, it did one good.'

CHAPTER XXX

AMONG THE BLIND

A Leader of the Blind—Honours—His Last Speech.

What he meant to the Blind.

What his happy, successful life meant to the blind, and how he heartened them by his hearty personality, cannot be overestimated.

'I went with him,' says Mr. Dryhurst, 'to a tea-meeting at Bethnal Green. It was night, and the Assembly Hall, which was low, was crowded with over one thousand blind people and their guides. Fawcett, who spoke briefly, was greeted with fervent enthusiasm when he entered, and when, in the course of the speech he exclaimed in his thundering voice, 'Do not wall us up in institutions, but let us live as other men live,' the excitement of the audience and the animation of the blind faces, was something which I shall never forget.'

A Leader out of Darkness.

While at Cambridge preparing this book, the writer was sent for by a blind lady whom she did not know. She was old and ill in bed, but in happier times she had known Fawcett, who had often dined at her house. Recently she also had lost her sight, and she evidently felt that she had a debt to the great blind man who had been her friend when she could see. She wished the relief of expressing her indebtedness, as in her weak voice she struggled to say: 'I wanted to tell you that in my life no one has helped me as much as Mr. Fawcett; his help is constant even now.'

Fawcett had always lived so that he might be strong and attain. He was careful of his diet, exercise and clothing; of this last to such a degree that his friends, as we know, loved to poke fun at him for his precautions against chills. Tradition tells of two suits of underclothing being superimposed while in an express train London-bound on his way to the Houses of Parliament.

We are given a glimpse of him at this time by a friend: 'Coming towards me I saw a man leaning on the arm of his companion, and walking with a smiling upturned face, as though he were watching the clouds of smoke from a small but exceedingly fragrant cigar.'

The Wear of Work.

He seemed now quite his old self again in mind and body, though he would often return home exhausted from his work, and when Mrs. Fawcett read to him he would frequently fall fast asleep. On one occasion she was reading to him the biography of some distinguished man, and had come to a passage where the author was describing a moonlight scene, when Fawcett, waking from a nap, interrupted the peaceful picture with the exclamation, 'I always said he was a sagacious old fool.'

Honours.

It was natural that when his achievements had won him such wide popularity and distinction he should receive many of those tokens which most men cherish. Oxford gave him the honorary degree of Doctor of Civil Law; Würzburg, on its tricentenary celebration, made him Doctor of Political Economy; he was elected a corresponding member of the section of political economy of the Institute of France; the Royal Society elected him to a Fellowship, and in 1883, a year after his illness, the University of Glasgow gave him an LL.D. and elected him their Lord Rector, the other candidates being Lord Bute and Mr. Ruskin.

He did not live to give his Rectorial address, but Mrs. Fawcett sent a copy of his Hackney speech to each of the students, saying as preface, 'This last speech appears to me so characteristic of him on whom the choice of the students fell, so free from party passion and prejudice, so scrupulously just to opponents, so fearless in saying what he knew would not be popular, so instinct with devotion to principle and love of justice, that I cannot believe it will be useless or unacceptable to young men just beginning the battle of life.'

His friends had been over sanguine in their belief in Fawcett's restored strength. He did not take a proper vacation in the summer of 1884, but devoted himself to settling questions which he found anxious and onerous about telephone rights. The work told on his weakened constitution. In September he went to Wales, 'made a vigorous little speech,' and visited two friends. He returned for his lectures at Cambridge, but he was forced to be much in London. Even so he snatched every occasion for fresh air and exercise that he could. He gloried in the great out-of-doors.

Bells.

One Sunday he went rowing with a friend on the Thames. It was a glorious day, and Fawcett was delighted with the church bells. They paused to listen, and he exclaimed, 'How lovely the bells are!' and then added wickedly, 'and how glad I am that I am not in church.' About him there always hovered a glint of the impish schoolboy playing 'hookey,' especially when he was in the open air, revelling in the warmth of the sunshine, listening to the lap and swish of the water, the rustle of the leaves, the wind in the grass, or the songs of the birds. He loved all these glad noises, and at such times his whole being gave out joy, his gay spirit had the freshness and the unhesitating truthfulness of early youth. He was so full of the light of that inner eye which nothing could darken, that he forgot his blindness in the fulness of his own bright soul. Heartily would he have assented to the sentiment: 'It is a comely fashion to be glad—Joy is the grace we say to God.' It surprised and startled those about him, whom he made so oblivious of his misfortune, when he would ask, 'Is the sun shining?'

Golden Leaves of Autumn.

Hearing that the foliage at Clarendon was singularly lovely that autumn, the tired, busy, blind man snatched a moment to run down to see the woods. The glory of that autumn light on the trees at Salisbury, when he was last permitted to see them, was never to be forgotten. He refused to remember the catastrophe which had blinded him, and still delighted to recall the beauty thus lost, and to love all similar autumn glories.

His Last Speech.

His final speech was made at Hackney on 13th October; he lectured with weakened voice on the 30th, went to London, and returned to Cambridge, where, though he found the weather damp and raw, he enjoyed a ride with some relatives. In the evening he compared his cold with that of a friend who was dining with them, and was forced to admit that the friend's cold was superior to his own.

The next day, though he did Post Office work with his secretary, he kept his bed; his lecture for Monday had to be put off. On Tuesday and Wednesday he grew worse, though he greatly enjoyed Mrs. Fawcett's reading of Dickens, laughing heartily over it. It was now necessary to ask Lord Eversley, so often his able substitute, to act again as his deputy.

CHAPTER XXXI

LIGHT

The Passing—The People grieve—Sorrow in Parliament—The Nation's Loss—Letters from Queen Victoria, the Prince of Wales (the late King Edward) and Gladstone—The Railroad Men's Tribute—The Significance of his Life—India's Loss—Fawcett's Message.

Between the Lights.

On Thursday morning, 6th November 1884, the two doctors who saw him found that his heart was weak, and he asked his secretary to notify the papers of his illness. Another doctor came from London, and when the three went to Fawcett's room, they found that there was no hope of his recovery. Thoughtful as always of the comfort of others, he asked in a failing voice if dinner had been arranged for the doctor who had just come.

When his hands began to grow cold, he thought the weather had changed. Practical and exact to the last, he said: 'The best things to warm my hands with would be my fur gloves. They are in the pocket of my coat in the dressing-room.' He never spoke again. In the quiet room, the dull autumn afternoon darkened as his wife and daughter sat by the bedside. Very gently, his brave fight won, the tired blind man's unquenchable spirit left them in the twilight and passed to find the light.

Remembered and Loved.

Rarely has a loss caused so much deep personal sorrow in every class. A dearly loved friend of many had gone, a noble life had been spent for others. There was mourning in many a little cottage when the head of the family read aloud that the good Postmaster-General had passed away.

In the misty lamplit village squares, and in the market-place at Salisbury, the rural labourers gathered to lament his loss, and to recall his many good deeds and the countless little friendlinesses which he had personally shown to so many of them.

'That such a man should have died at only fifty-one is one of those apparent wastes in Nature before which our philosophy stands impotent; but that such a light should have existed at all makes philosophy superfluous in contemplating it.'[4]

The morning after Fawcett's going, Lady Courtney told the news to her par-lourmaid, who had known Fawcett. On entering the kitchen, to her surprise the cook burst out weeping and sat by the table rocking herself to and fro. 'Why,' said Lady Courtney, 'Maria, you didn't know Mr. Fawcett, did you?' 'Ah, yes, your ladyship, I knew him, the kind gentleman. It was when you and his lordship were out of town. I opened the door for him, and when he found you were not at home, he said, "I have been here to dine very often, and I want to know you." "Oh no, sir," says I, "I'm only the cook," with which he puts out his hand and shakes mine like an old friend, as he says, "Well, I'm very glad indeed to meet you." Then I offered him a glass of water, ma'am, which he drank so grateful.' Lady Courtney queried, 'But Maria, why didn't you offer him tea, for the credit of the house?' 'Oh, your ladyship, I didn't dare to, for fear he'd see the state of the house with your ladyship away.'

When the news came to the House of Commons, sudden as such news always is, it fell to the Marquis of Hartington to announce it to the House. It is said that he all but broke down.

Sorrow in Parliament.

Later in the evening there were more formal expressions of grief. Sir Stafford Northcote, on behalf of the Conservative Party, whom Fawcett had so consistent-ly opposed, spoke of the loss the House had sustained, and said: 'I do not think anybody can recall a single word that ever fell from him that gave unnecessary offence or pain to any one.' The Marquis of Hartington, on behalf of the Govern-ment, said Fawcett commanded the 'respect, I think I may say the affection, of the whole House'; and Mr. Justin McCarthy, on behalf of the Irish Party, spoke with much feeling of 'the sudden and melancholy close of so promising and great a career.' The next evening Gladstone, who had not been present the night before, said: 'Mr. Fawcett's name is a name which is heard in all quarters of the House with feelings of the greatest respect. We have all been accustomed to regard with admiration his admirable integrity and independence of mind, his absolute de-votion to the public service, the marvellous tenacity of his memory, combined with his remarkable clearness of mental vision; and, I think, even above all these, if possible, the rare courage, the unfailing, the unmeasured courage, with which he confronted and mastered all the difficulties which would have daunted and repelled an ordinary man in connection with the loss of the precious gift of sight. From these and other causes he acquired a place in the hearts and minds such as is undoubtedly accorded to few; and I believe that he had won a place equally high in the esteem and respect of the House of Commons. I wish in these few words to place on record, in the name of myself and my colleagues, our deep sense of the loss of a most distinguished public servant.' The last words were spoken by Lord John Manners, who, referring to the personal intercourse he had had with Fawcett, said, 'It was impossible to exceed in courtesy and fairness the eminent statesman whose loss we all deplore.'

---

[4] This tribute is from an American appreciator of Fawcett.

Writing of Fawcett shortly after his death, Mr. Beresford Hope used these words: 'He was a man who had conquered all personal enmity, all personal suspicion, and lived in the hearts of every man, on every side of the House, without exception. Ask me why it was? That is a difficult question to answer. The appreciation of character—the influence that a man has—is generally indescribable.... He had gained a strange influence over the House, from the absolute certainty with which he inspired every man of the clear, transparent honesty and courage of his character.'

The Reason of a Boy.

Fawcett was always strongly opposed to taking away any legitimate pleasure, and the keen appreciation of this fact by a child seems worth recording. Soon after the Postmaster's death, his small nephew, who had been promised that he should go to the Lord Mayor's Show, begged to be taken there; the family naturally hesitated, and discussed the propriety of the boy's going to the festivity the day before his uncle's funeral. The natural question was, 'What would Fawcett have said under similar circumstances?' The small nephew piped up with 'I know Uncle Harry would have said: "Go, my boy!"' This was so true that the boy went.

Britain mourns.

Numerous letters were sent to the family, some from those who, from lack of learning, were forced to dictate their letters to the village schoolmaster. Others, who had rarely struggled with the intricate problems of pen and paper, strove painfully to put their sympathy into written words. Telegrams and resolutions of sympathy came from workingmen's societies, labour unions, and all kinds of associations and societies, tokens of love and grief from a vaster circle of personal friends than almost any one ever had.

We have the privilege of printing a facsimile of the sympathetic letter written with her own hand by Queen Victoria, and of the note of condolence from the Prince of Wales (the late King Edward).

Letters from Queen Victoria and the Prince of Wales (the late King Edward).

'BALMORAL CASTLE,
'*November 8th, 1884.*

'DEAR MRS. FAWCETT,—I am anxious to express to you myself the true and sincere sympathy I feel for you in your present terrible bereavement, as well as my sincere regret for the loss of your distinguished husband, who bore his great trial with such courage and patience, and who served his Queen and country ably and faithfully.

'You, who were so devoted a wife to him, must, even in this hour of overwhelming grief, be gratified by the universal expression of respect and regret on this sad occasion.

'That He Who alone can give consolation and peace in the

hour of affliction may support you, is the earnest wish of yours sincerely,

'(Signed) VICTORIA, R. AND I.'

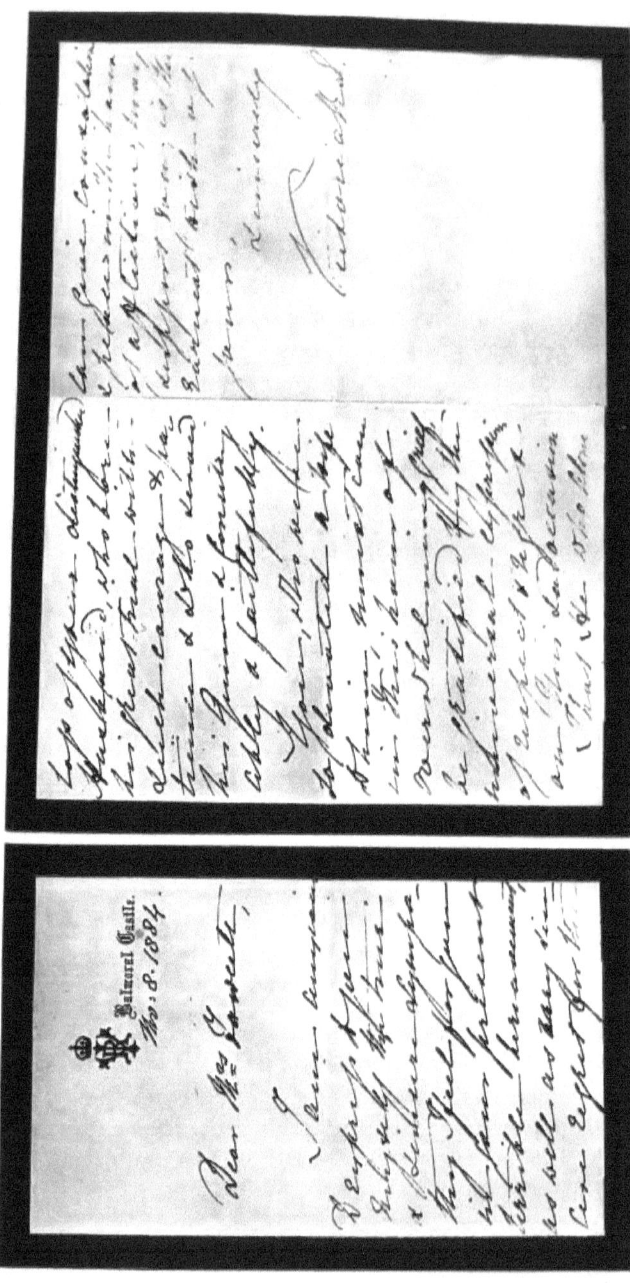

FACSIMILE OF A LETTER FROM QUEEN VICTORIA TO MRS. FAWCETT.

'Sandringham,

'King's Lynn, November 8th, 1884.

'Dear Mrs. Fawcett,—You are certain to receive many letters expressing sympathy with your present grief, and although I hardly like intruding so soon on your great sorrow, yet I am anxious to express how deeply both the Princess and myself sympathise with you in this severe hour of trial. Mr. Fawcett cannot fail to be deeply mourned and regretted by all who knew him—but he has left a name, which will ever be remembered among England's distinguished men.—Believe me, dear Mrs. Fawcett, truly yours,

'(Signed) Albert Edward.'

SANDRINGHAM.
KING'S LYNN.

November 8th 1884.

Dear Mrs Fawcett,

You are certain to receive many letters expressing sympathy with your present grief. And although I should dislike intruding so soon on your great sorrow

[...] yet I am anxious to express how deeply both the Princess & myself sympathize with you in this severe hour of trial. Mr Fawcett cannot fail to be deeply mourned & regretted by [...]

[...] who knew him. And he has left a name which will be ever remembered among England's distinguished sons.

Believe me,
Dear Mrs Fawcett
Truly yours,
Albert Edward

FACSIMILE OF A LETTER FROM THE PRINCE OF WALES (KING EDWARD VII) TO MRS. FAWCETT

What Gladstone wrote.

Mr. Gladstone wrote to Fawcett's father. Miss Fawcett has kindly given us permission to reprint the letter.

'10 Downing Street,
'Whitehall, *November 25th, 1884.*

'Dear Sir,—Will you allow me to intrude upon you for a moment by offering to you in private my assurances of deep sympathy under the grievous loss you have sustained, and to repeat also the testimony which I have endeavoured to render in public to your distinguished son. There has been no public man in our day whose remarkable qualities have been more fully recognised by his fellow-countrymen, and more deeply enshrined in their memories. There they will long remain now that they form the subject of recollection only and are no longer associated, as they were until the sad event, with sanguine and brilliant hopes.

'He has left a record of some qualities which are given to few; but of others, perhaps yet more remarkable, which all his fellow-countrymen may in their degree emulate and follow; for integrity so high, and courage so far beyond the common range, aid more often than his great powers of intellect and memory to profitable imitation, and will, I trust, give to thousands a powerful incentive to honourable imitation and a means of real advancement.

'Heartily wishing to you, dear Sir, both in retrospect and in prospect every consolation,—I remain, faithfully yours,

'W. E. Gladstone.
'W. Fawcett, Esqr.'

Mr. Fawcett, senior, died at Salisbury at the ripe age of ninety-five, after a successful and much honoured life.

It is interesting to read what the Prime Minister said of Fawcett, by whom he had been at times so vigorously and successfully opposed, and to whom the downfall of his Government was once largely due.

The Old Folk and Salisbury.

The sorrow of the grief-stricken parents in Salisbury for the loss of their beloved son seemed too great a burden for their aged shoulders to bear. But slowly, as time went on, the father gathered comfort from the sympathy of great and humble. Reviewing lovingly bit by bit the brave course which his boy had run, he realised perhaps, as the crowning comfort, that in the inscrutable workings of fate, his unwittingly blinding his own child had not after all proved an irreparable calamity. Rather it had, by depriving the lad of the blessing of sight, miraculously sped him on valiantly to a great life gladly lived.

From Carpenters, Bricklayers, etc.

Among the many sympathetic letters sent to Mrs. Fawcett, perhaps none express more truly the feelings of those to whom her husband had given his constant solicitude, and certainly none are more touching, than these two:—

PANGBOURNE, *November 8th, 1884.*

'DEAR MADAM,—I hope you will forgive us, but having followed the political life of the late Professor Fawcett, we felt when we saw his death in the papers on the 7th that we had lost a personal friend, and that a great man had gone from us. The loss to you must be beyond measure; but we as part of the nation do give you who have been his helper our heartfelt sympathy in your great trouble, and we do hope you may find a little consolation in knowing that his work that he has done for the working classes has not been in vain.

'We, as working men, do offer you and your child our deepest sympathy, and beg to be yours respectfully,

'HARRY COX, Carpenter.
CHARLES EDDY, Carpenter.
RICHARD BOWLES, Carpenter.
G. LEWENDON, Bricklayer.
GEORGE BROWN, Bricklayer.
WILLIAM COX, Carpenter.
CHARLES COX, Blacksmith.
M. CLIFFORD, Postmaster.
F. CLIFFORD, Clerk.'

A Tribute from the Railroad men of Brighton.

'11 ELDER PLACE,
'BRIGHTON, *November 11th, 1884.*

'DEAR MRS. FAWCETT,—Excuse me in not writing you sooner, on the sad death of your dear lamented husband. Several of his old friends at the Brighton Railway Works has wished me to ask you privately how you are situated in a pecuniary sense. We always thought that the Professor was a poor man, and only had what he earned by his talents; his three years of office could not have brought in much money for you and the family to live in ease and comfort for the rest of your days. It is our opinion that you are richly entitled to a public pension.

'Failing this, would you accept a public subscription, say a penny one, from the working classes of this country, for the many good and noble deeds your noble partner done for the working classes of this country. His advice was always sound, good and practical, and full of sympathy, a good private friend to all men.

'I see you had a plentiful supply of flowers, but those flowers soon fade and are no support to the poor and fatherless ones. I am confident, if you could make up your mind to accept a penny testimonial the working classes would give cheerfully, not in the shape of charity, but for public and striking services rendered by one of the best men since Edmund Burke. We only wish he had lived twenty years longer.

'Pray excuse my plain way of writing to you, as an honest workman, one of his supporters from first to last. His last letter to me a month back was full of sound and good advice concerning our Provident Society.—Believe me, your sincere friend and well-wisher,

JOHN SHORT, Senior.'

Mrs. Fawcett, profoundly touched by this letter, was able to say that she could not properly accept the generous offer, as her husband had left her adequately provided for. Mr. Short, who had written the letter, replied to Mrs. Fawcett, 'our men of the railway works say that you are entitled to all honour for refusing a pension or a public subscription from the working men; also that your dear husband and our best friend has practised what he always preached to us, private thrift!'

Burial.

Fawcett was buried in the churchyard at Trumpington, near Cambridge, by the little old church, with its square tower, which he had so often passed on his joyful walks and rides. He was followed to his resting-place by representatives of all the classes and the peoples who had loved him. Those humble folk who were so dear to him mingled with statesmen of all parties and many countries, delegates from learned bodies and universities, his colleagues, and the undergraduates from his beloved Cambridge.

The significance of Fawcett's life.

The influence of such a career, the significance of its eternal echo, grows in value each year. As life becomes more complicated, and competition keener, men in the general struggle naturally think themselves forced to safeguard their own interests, and forget what, by their very birthright as citizens, they owe to the community, to the making and purifying of the Government which should be the protector of the weak, the instigator of progress, and the guardian of national honour.

Fawcett's life awakens us to the possibilities of happiness and usefulness without the aid of money or position, and even despite one of the gravest impediments under which a man can labour. He completely forgot himself and his personal interests, and in so doing found happiness and success. His career was a forceful illustration of that ancient truth, 'He that loses his life shall find it.'

His heroic victory should help to give that faith and inspiration needed so much in our day in every field. Like that great friend of liberty with whom he so deeply sympathised and to whom we have compared him, Fawcett came from the humble people whom he fully appreciated, and he too might have said that 'God must have loved the plain people, or He would not have made so many of them.' He too struggled against gigantic difficulties, and became a leader of his country-men. From this position of vantage, which he cherished because it enabled him to do good effectively, he helped the poor and neglected, and those who had no voice to ask justice for themselves. Even the least of these touched his great heart and claimed his sympathy, and he wrought unsparingly, unselfishly for their rights. Worn out with his ceaseless task, he too was taken in his prime, at the height of his powers, beloved and reverenced by his own people, and the great and small of many lands.

MEMORIAL IN WESTMINSTER ABBEY

Gloria Mundis.

A national memorial and many others were set up. Contributions were re-ceived from all parts of the Empire, in gifts ranging from the widow's mite to the munificent donations of Indian princes, in recognition of the help which Fawcett had given to their country. To the one fittingly placed in Westminster Abbey, the employees of the Post Office contributed one-quarter of the cost. Besides the portrait, the memorial includes two figures symbolising Brotherhood, and others for Zeal, Justice, Fortitude, Sympathy and Industry.

The remainder of the National Memorial Fund was devoted to the Fawcett Scholarship, available for blind students at the universities, and to the Fawcett playgrounds, gymnasium, skating rinks, boating equipment, and other athletic facilities at the Royal Normal College for the Blind.

India's loss.

We have spoken of the feeling of India. A great public meeting was held at Bombay; extracts from some of the speeches are given below, and with them some cuttings from the Indian papers.

'This great assembly is here to do honour to the memory of a high-minded English statesman, whose name has become a household word out here, to express that policy of strict justice and warm sympathy which alone can bind India to England.'

'The best friend of India has gone—the Right Honble. Henry Fawcett. All people will regret the death of this statesman—especially those in India. He had so identified himself with the interests of India, and so fearlessly advocated the cause of the dumb millions of this poor country, that he had gained for himself the honorary title of the Member for India. It was certainly unfortunate that he had no place in the Cabinet. His colleagues, who knew him thoroughly, were probably afraid that in Indian matters he would prove too stiff for them. By far the best place for him would have been that of Secretary of State for India. In fact, ever since he was Postmaster-General India lost the services of its Member.'

'Independently of his political services to India, Mr. Fawcett was well known among us as an author. His *Manual of Political Economy* has become a text-book in all our colleges and universities, and his other writings on social and economic questions are extensively read by the educated portion of our countrymen.'

'There was no more touching spectacle than that of the blind Professor devoting himself as the champion of the country he had never seen, and the steadfast friend of the people with whom he had never come into personal contact, simply because that country needed a champion, and those people wanted a friend to represent their interests. Such a figure strikes me as even more chivalrous than the figures of the ideal knights who went about redressing human wrongs.'

'To India his loss is truly irreparable.'

The Statue in his Birthplace.

'In the market-place at Salisbury, near the house where Fawcett was born, and where he made his first economic investigation, they have placed a statue of him, so that the inhabitants of India and others coming from distant parts to see Stonehenge and the great Cathedral may pause before the memorial, and, seeing Fawcett's name, will remember that he was the friend who fought for their rights.'

His Message.

As a friend wrote when deploring Fawcett's untimely death: 'The necessity of the hour is one brave man, faithful to his convictions, strong enough to make himself heard above the angry cries of a mob, and determined that no amount of popular applause, no momentary party advantage, no miserable plea of expediency, and no false imputation of cowardice shall move him one hair's-breadth from the path of rectitude.' Yes, Fawcett is needed to-day, and his example is needed now — the teaching of his generous brotherhood, his intense industry, his fair thoroughness of investigation, and his conscientious deliberation.

On his grave they have written, 'Speak to the people that they go forward.' In obedience to this summons this book has been written, and in hope that it will lead others to tell the story over and over again. It may too help others to follow in the footsteps of this country boy, who, blinded, fought valiantly against tremendous odds, and taught himself to ignore his misfortune and to make at last his spirit see so clearly that he found the truth and pointed it out to others. He became the champion of those who most needed a protector, and battled against oppression, ignorance, and neglect. He gave to the humblest the right to enjoy the commons and forests which he himself could not see. He strove for the friendless in India, and for the poor woman who had no voice in the making of the laws which bound her. He shouldered tasks beyond his strength, loving them. He attained the best because he believed the best.

There is no parallel in history for this heroic and romantic life, in spite of the overhanging shadow, so full of usefulness, of joy and light. So keen was the sight of the eyes on his finger-tips, that he could detect the smallest leaf carried by the stream against his fishing-line. After a score of years he would recognise the laugh and the voice of a long absent friend. He worshipped in the cathedral of the immensity he could not see. His creed was simple, — love and service; sacrifice, his interpretation of God, and the secret of his life.

He was called the 'Messiah of the Blind,' and it was said that with his death the beacon for those who sit in darkness had been extinguished. Let us rather say that he kindled one for them for all time; that saving for the blindness of the spirit there is no blindness; through the light shed by his bright and noble life this blind man has proved it, and still teaches us to see.

HENRY FAWCETT FROM 'PUNCH

BORN 1833, DIED NOV. 6, 1884

Virtus in arducis! Valour against odds
That must have daunted courage less complete.
A spectacle to gladden men, and meet
The calm approval of the gazing gods.
So some large singer of the heroic days
Might well have summed that life the fatal shears
Too soon have severed. Many fruitful years,
More conquests yet, still wider meed of praise,
All hoped of him who had goodwill of all, —
The brave, the justly balanced, calmly strong,
Friend of all truth, and foe of every wrong,
Who now, whilst lingering autumn's last leaves fall,
Too soon! too soon! if the stern stroke of fate
Ever too early falls, or falls too late,
At least the passing of this stern, strong soul
In fullest strength and clearness wakes lament.
We could have better spared a hundred loud,
Incontinent, blaring flatterers of the crowd
Than him, whose self-respecting years were spent
In silent thought and sense-directed toil,
Ungagged by greed, unshackled and unswayed
By sordid impulse of the sophist's trade,
By lies unsnared and unseduced by spoil.
No braver conquest o'er ill fortune's flout
Our age has seen than his, who held straight on
Though the great God-gift from his days was gone,
'And wisdom at one entrance quite shut out.'
Held on with genial stoutness, seeing more
Than men with sight undarkened, but with mind
Through prejudice and party bias blind.
The 'foolish fires' of faction through the flare
Betraying beacons, in the battle's van.
Vale! A valid and a valiant man!
Ampler horizons and serener air
Await the fighter of so good a fight

Than favour Party's low, mist-haunted hollow.
Heart-deep regrets and honest plaudits follow
Him who has passed from darkness into light.

Punch.

MEMORIALS

APPENDIX

To make this record complete the following descriptions of the Fawcett Memorials is appended, together with the copy of a letter from Mrs. Fawcett's sister.

There are three memorials in London, besides others elsewhere.

The national memorial to Fawcett in Westminster Abbey bears the following inscription, written by Sir Leslie Stephen.

HENRY FAWCETT
BORN 26 AUGUST 1833. DIED 6 NOVEMBER 1884

After losing his sight by an accident, at the age of 24, he became Professor of Political Economy in the University of Cambridge, Member of four Parliaments, and from 1880 to 1884, H.M. Postmaster-General.

His inexorable fidelity to his convictions commanded the respect of statesmen. His chivalrous self-devotion to the cause of the poor and helpless won the affection of his countrymen and of his Indian fellow-subjects. His heroic acceptance of the calamity of blindness has left a memorable example of the power of a brave man to transmute evil into good and wrest victory from misfortune.

This memorial was erected by the subscribers to a national memorial.

Memorial Scholarship for the Blind. Playgrounds, skating rink, boats and other athletic equipment at the Royal Normal College for the Blind.

As has been said elsewhere, the national memorial in Westminster Abbey represented contributions received from all parts of the Empire. This sum was expended not only in erecting the memorial in Westminster Abbey, but also in providing the above-mentioned scholarship and athletic facilities for the blind.

The small Vauxhall Park, just behind Vauxhall Station, includes within its area the site of the house where Fawcett lived from shortly after his marriage till his death. In it stands a handsome memorial to Fawcett given by Sir Henry Doulton. The high pedestal is decorated with eight panels in bas-relief. Fawcett is represented seated. An angel stands behind his chair and is about to crown him with a wreath of laurel. The inscription is the same as that in Westminster Abbey.

A drinking fountain was erected as a Women's Memorial to Fawcett in the Gardens on the Thames Embankment, east of Charing Cross.

'The first person to drink of the waters of the fountain was a postman; this gracefully recalled the regard in which Professor Fawcett was held by the humble servants of the state, whose duties he regulated, and whose welfare he had ever at heart during his tenure of the office of Postmaster-General.'—Extract from a contemporaneous paper.

A memorial was placed by the inhabitants of Alderburgh in the Parish Church there. The words with which the memorial is inscribed are as follow:

Erected by the inhabitants of Alderburgh
In memory of the Rt. Hon. Henry Fawcett, M.P.,
who was born August 26, 1833, and who
died November 6, 1884.
His brave and kindly nature will ever live in
the hearts of all who knew and loved him.
Be ye also strong, and of good courage.

There is a memorial window in Trumpington Church; below the figures of Truth, Fortitude and Charity is the inscription:

In memory of
HENRY FAWCETT
Born August 26, 1833
Died November 6, 1884

A statue of Fawcett was erected to his memory in the market-place of Salisbury, near the house where he was born.

EXTRACT FROM A LETTER FROM MRS. FAWCETT'S SISTER

'A clergyman came to me one day in the street and asked if I was not Mrs. Fawcett's sister. I said "Yes," and then he told me his little story.

'A friend of his had become blind and had lost hope and courage, and seemed unable to face the disaster; then some one reminded him of Mr. Fawcett, and read his life to him, and the poor man took fresh heart, and met his misfortune bravely. The clergyman added, "I do not know Mrs. Fawcett or any of his family, and could not let slip this chance of telling them what Mr. Fawcett's example had done for my friend."'

May his example continue ceaselessly to help, and may this little book make his story more widely known, so that those who sit in darkness may see the light which his keen spirit saw—and seeing, choose the nobler part.

INDEX

I

J

K

L

Lector House believes that a society develops through a two-fold approach of continuous learning and adaptation, which is derived from the study of classic literary works spread across the historic timeline of literature records. Therefore, we aim at reviving, repairing and redeveloping all those inaccessible or damaged but historically as well as culturally important literature across subjects so that the future generations may have an opportunity to study and learn from past works to embark upon a journey of creating a better future.

This book is a result of an effort made by Lector House towards making a contribution to the preservation and repair of original ancient works which might hold historical significance to the approach of continuous learning across subjects.

HAPPY READING & LEARNING!

LECTOR HOUSE LLP
E-MAIL: lectorpublishing@gmail.com